# MARQUETTE UNIVERSITY
## SLAVIC INSTITUTE

# SHEVCHENKO MEETS AMERICA

By

ROMAN SMAL-STOCKI

*"The Pursuit of Truth to Make Men Free"*

MARQUETTE UNIVERSITY
SLAVIC INSTITUTE
MILWAUKEE, WISCONSIN
1964

THIRD EDITION

Library of Congress Catalog Card Number: 64-20248

PRINTED IN U.S.A.

# DEDICATION

to the memory of
the 34th successor of
George Washington

## PRESIDENT JOHN FITZGERALD KENNEDY

who was slain by a Communist
and
as an expression of deep gratitude to the
Honorable Senators and Congressmen who
sponsored the House Joint Resolution 311
during the 86th Congress, and to

## PRESIDENT DWIGHT D. EISENHOWER

who signed it into Public Law 86-749 on
September 13, 1960:

SENATOR LYNDON B. JOHNSON OF TEXAS
CONGRESSMAN ALVIN M. BENTLEY OF MICHIGAN
CONGRESSMAN EDWARD J. DERWINSKI OF ILLINOIS
SENATOR THOMAS J. DODD OF CONNECTICUT
SENATOR EVERETT M. DIRKSEN OF ILLINOIS
CONGRESSMAN THADDEUS J. DULSKI OF NEW YORK
CONGRESSMAN MICHAEL A. FEIGHAN OF OHIO
CONGRESSMAN DANIEL J. FLOOD OF PENNSYLVANIA
SENATOR THEODORE F. GREEN OF RHODE ISLAND
SENATOR JACOB JAVITS OF NEW YORK
CONGRESSMAN PAUL C. JONES OF MISSOURI
SENATOR KENNETH B. KEATING OF NEW YORK
CONGRESSMAN JOHN LESINSKI OF MICHIGAN
CONGRESSMAN JOHN W. MCCORMACK OF MASSACHUSETTS

ACKNOWLEDGMENTS

Particular thanks are presented to the following persons, institutions and publishing companies for permission to use their illustrations:

The Sterling Library, Yale University, for the portrait of Washington Irving;

The Detroit Institute of Arts for the photograph of Shevchenko's bust by A. Archipenko;

The Public Library, New York City, for the picture of Robert Fulton's steamboat from Alexander Anderson's Scrapbooks;

The New York Historical Society for the picture of Robert Fulton;

The University of California Press, Berkeley, for the illustration of Catalpa from *Ornamental Trees* by Evelyn Maino and Frances Howard, illustrated by Evelyn Maino, 1955; and

to Dr. Theodor Luciw for the photograph of Rev. A. Honcharenko in Alaska.

## Preface

THIS current year of 1964 is the 150th birthday anniversary of Taras Shevchenko, the bard of Ukraine.

With the support of the American and other free world delegates to the United Nations, UNESCO has dedicated this entire year to the observance of commemorations to be held throughout the world in honor of Shevchenko. This is without doubt the highest testimonial which could be given to attest to Shevchenko's universal significance for all mankind. The action taken by the world organization holds a special significance for Americans whose founder and first president, George Washington, provided the inspiration for Shevchenko in his fight for liberty for all victims of Russian autocracy and imperialism.

The United States Congress contributed an unforgettable page in the history of American-Slavic relations when by unanimous vote it passed Public Law 86-749, which was later approved by President Dwight D. Eisenhower on September 13, 1960, authorizing the erection of a statue of Taras Shevchenko on public grounds in our national capital, Washington, D.C. The monument, to be placed on 22nd and P streets, N.W., will be unveiled during special ceremonies on June 27, 1964.

The Slavic Institute of Marquette University, Milwaukee, Wis., pays honor to this anniversary by publishing this Paper No. 18, prepared by its Director, Dr. Roman Smal-Stocki, who is also President of the Shevchenko Memorial Committee of America, Inc.

This Paper brings to Americans, especially to Americans of Slavic descent, little known information about the ideological influences which our Founding Father, George Washington, had on the Ukrainian bard and about the influence that the ideas contained in the Declaration of Independence had on ensuing developments in the political life of Eastern Europe.

This Paper, coming as it does at a time when the same problems which faced Shevchenko are still pressing, will be widely welcomed.

Milwaukee, Wisconsin
March 15, 1964

Alfred J. Sokolnicki
Slavic Institute

# SHEVCHENKO MEETS AMERICA

## I

### Introduction
### Taras Shevchenko

UKRAINE, the second largest Slavic nation, presently enslaved by Russian Communist imperialism, contributed a great poet to world literature—Taras Shevchenko (1814-1861).

Shevchenko's greatness can be grasped only with the proper understanding of the historical background of Ukraine and of all Europe as well and, above all, of Shevchenko's own unhappy and rather brief life.

Shevchenko's life was truly one of dedication and tragedy. Born in the Ukrainian village of Moryntsi, he was the son of a serf of Baron Engelhardt. From early childhood he showed talent for drawing. His master, the Baron, who had used him as a pageboy, sent him to study with the Italian painter, Lampi, in Warsaw. Later Baron Engelhardt took the young Shevchenko to St. Petersburg where enthusiastic admirers of his talent bought his freedom for 2,500 rubles. Shevchenko next entered the St. Petersburg Imperial Academy of Fine Arts around which were gathered at that time the artistic and intellectual elite of the empire. It was here that Shevchenko became a favorite pupil of the great painter, Karl Bryulov (1799-1852). It was here, too, that he completed his education with distinction by earning the Academy medal. Shevchenko's industry and thirst for knowledge led him to supplement his studies by extensive readings of the works of Dante, Chateaubriand, Victor Hugo, Goethe, Schiller, Heine, Mickiewicz, and especially of the translated works of William Shakespeare, of Lord Byron, of Dickens, and Scott, and by the study of the French language. The ideas of Mazzini and his celebrated disciple, Garibaldi, were also to deeply influence him.

Self Portrait of Taras Shevchenko presented to Princess Barbara Repnin (1843).

There, in the far, foggy, and cold north of St. Petersburg, homesick for his sunny and colorful Ukraine, which the great Polish poet Slowacki called the Greece of the Slavic world, Shevchenko started to write poetry and with the help of friends he published *Kobzar, (The Minstrel,)* in 1840, a book which even today can be found in every Ukrainian home. While visiting his oppressed native land later, Shevchenko was fortunate enough to be befriended by Princess Barbara Repnin, the granddaughter of the last Hetman of Ukraine, Rozumovsky.

Shevchenko's romanticism, glorifying the lost freedom and statehood of Ukraine, permeated his works and fostered revolutionary ideas against the Russian political and social regimes. Widely circulated throughout Ukraine, Shevchenko's bold ideas stimulated in Ukrainian people anew the spirit of revolutionary and conspiratorial nationalism. Shevchenko was subsequently denounced by the Russian authorities, arrested, and then, without a court trial, punished by Emperor Tsar Nicholas I. His sentence was to serve as a private at a military barracks on the border of Russian Asia. The exiled Shevchenko carried with him the Tsar's personally written orders: "Shevchenko be placed under strict guard, writing and drawing prohibited."

The 10 years from 1847 to 1857 were a terrible void in the poet's life. He survived by memorizing large parts of the New Testament, by meeting with Polish revolutionaries who were also exiled there, and through the support given him by sympathetic officers and friends. Following the death of Tsar Nicholas I, Shevchenko was granted amnesty by his successor, Tsar Alexander II, and he returned to St. Petersburg a broken man soon to die. He was welcomed back as a symbol of resistance to autocracy and as a prophet of liberty.

The Tomb of Taras Shevchenko with the Memorial Cross
before the Revolution.

When Shevchenko died, his funeral was a gigantic demonstration from St. Petersburg to Ukraine of the people's hatred of their Russian enslavement. According to Shevchenko's "Testament," he was buried on a hill at Kaniv on the bank of the Dnieper. His grave became a national shrine dedicated to the idea of Ukrainian liberty and is still today continuously visited by pilgrims from all over the country.

The Russian Communists have since removed the huge iron cross that had been placed atop the hill as a symbol of Shevchenko's and his people's belief in the hope of Christianity which is embodied in the Crucifixion and Resurrection. They have replaced the cross with a tall obelisk monument to Shevchenko thus directing its propaganda to a systematic falsification to Shevchenko's works and the ideals which burned within them.

The Tomb of Taras Shevchenko with His Statue after the Communist Occupation.

## *Shevchenko's Mother Country's History*

VOLTAIRE excellently summed up the content of Ukrainian history in his *The History of Charles XII of Sweden* when he wrote: “Ukraine always aspired to liberty. (L’Ukraine a toujours aspiré à être libre.”) Partly because of her geopolitical location Ukraine suffered a fate similar to that of Ireland or Poland.

In the year 1654 the independent Ukrainian Cossack Republic, whose traditions were rooted in the glorious past of the Kievan Rus-Ukraine Kingdom (which lasted from the tenth to the thirteenth centuries) was linked by Hetman Chmelnicky with the dynasty of the Muscovite Tsars by his commitment to union in order to oppose Poland. The agreement reserved for Ukraine the status of a republic which was to have freely elected Hetmans and the right to conduct her own foreign policy.

Map of Ukraine. Atlas Johann Baptist Homann, Nuernberg 1710

Ukraine learned soon enough the meaning that the Muscovites placed on coexistence. So Chmelnicky’s successors attempted to abolish this Muscovite tie through a series of actions. First, Hetman Vyhovsky tried by re-establishing the Union of

Ukraine with Poland-Lithuania in Hadiach (1658); then Hetman Doroshenko preferred the establishment of the protectorate of Turkey over Ukraine to the tie with Muscovy (1671), and finally Hetman Mazepa tried it by concluding the alliance with Charles XII of Sweden. The guiding idea of Hetman Mazepa, who was immortalized by the poet, Lord Byron, and of his followers was that Ukraine should form a common anti-Russian front with Sweden which then included Finland, Estonia, and Latvia, and with the other neighboring nations of Poland-Lithuania, with the Don Cossacks, and with Turkey backed in the West by France. Only such a block could stop the aggressive imperialism of Tsar Peter I, into northwestern, western, and southern Europe.

But the results of the battle of Poltava in 1709, one of the 15 decisive battles of world history along with such battles as Marathon, Chalon, Hastings, Blenheim, Saratoga, and Waterloo,[1] were in favor of Russian Asiatic despotism. As a result the whole history of Europe up to the present time has undergone a tragic turn, leading to the domination of Eastern Europe by Russian imperialism. Later on, Catherine II, who together with Prussia and Austria partitioned the Polish-Lithuanian Commonwealth, abolished the last symbols of Ukrainian statehood: the Sich Army and the Hetmanate. She also condemned the peasantry into serfdom, confiscated the property of the Ukrainian Orthodox church and disposed Ukraine of all self rule by 1783.

The last Hetman to serve Ukraine was Rozumovsky to whose descendant, the later Russian Ambassador to Vienna, were dedicated some of Ludwig van Beethoven's compositions.

Thus was Ukraine finally integrated into the fast growing monster of Russian imperialism. It was this rampaging imperialism which swelled the area covered by Muscovite-Russian domination from 8.5 million square kilometers in 1600 to 22.2 million square kilometers in 1900. In the period 1812 to 1815 one-sixth of the earth's surface was one vast empire stretching as it did from Kalish in Poland to San Francisco in America.

This fantastic cancerous growth of Russian absolutism and imperialism in Europe and Asia, which even today is working to establish a foothold in Africa and America, was only possible

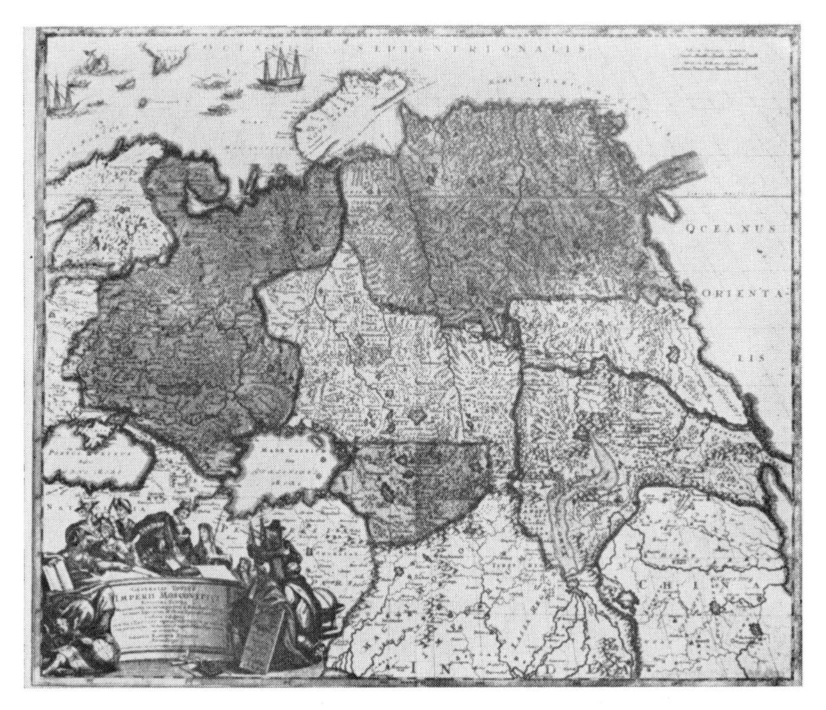


Map of Imperium Moscoviticum, later 1721 by Tsar Peter I renamed Russian Empire, Atlas Johann Baptist Homann, Nuernberg 1710

because of those events which occurred in Europe after the unsuccessful campaign of Napoleon against Moscow in 1812. It was this campaign which brought about Napoleon's collapse at Leipzig and his final defeat at Waterloo.

Tsar Alexander's role in Napoleon's defeat gave Russia a dominant position in Europe and a great importance in world politics since Russia stood as an autocratic rival of Great Britain which was dedicated to the parliamentarian system. The dark age of Metternichism then was free to embrace a large part of Europe which it did through the years up to 1848. Backed by the Holy Alliance of the three autocracies of Austria, Prussia, and Russia, this period represents the darkest reaction of divine right absolutism. This alliance stood as a monstrous force against the revolutionary demands of the oppressed nations for constitutions and parliamentarian rule. At Muenchengraetz (1833) the alliance was even further strengthened to make liberal movements totally impossible. They were forced to go underground.

Following the collapse of the Decembrist insurrection on December 25, 1825, Tsar Nicholas I, the "gendarme of Europe," began a rule which lasted to 1855. He crushed the Polish Revolt of 1830 and the Hungarian Revolt of 1848. His rule brought into the Russian Empire a complete intellectual suffocation, police terror, and censorship over literature, the press, and education.

Tsar Nicholas I's rule was, in fact, Russian Metternichism, the muzzling of all the nationalities of the empire. In this divine right absolute monarch was vested the total power of the Russian terrifying police state which made possible the development of the "Uvarov formula," a clear cut ideology and program for this sinister regime, called by the Russian historians, "Nikolayevshchina." Figuratively, this program was built on three pillars: Russian autocracy, Russian nationality or chauvinism, and Russian Orthodoxy.[2] With these principles then all the non-Russian nationalities, which constituted the majority of the population, had to be Russified—"Orthodoxized"—and converted into obedient serfs of Russian absolutism.

The resistance offered by the Russian liberal forces was rather weak. Only outside the Russian empire could Alexander Herzen, a half-German who lived from 1812 to 1870, publish in London *The Bell* and *The Northern Star,* attacking the "Byzantine-Prussian tyranny" of Tsar Nicholas I. Herzen characterized Nicholas' regime as "extreme brutality, cynicism, and inhumanity" by noting that it was "beyond the scope of ordinary language to express the plight of the common man."[3] This same token success outside Russian was also accomplished by the turbulent anarchist, Michael Bakunin (1814-1876), a forerunner of Russian bolshevism.[4]

Within the empire the "Westerners," the champions of Herzen, had little to say and all the influences of the German philosophers Fichte, Schelling, and Hegel only served to strengthen Russian chauvinism.

However, a bomb exploded within the Russian empire in 1836 when Peter Chaadayev (1794-1856) managed to publish his *Philosophical Letters* in Moscow which reflected a deep despair about the destiny of Russia in world history because she had neither a national idea nor a national goal. Chaadayev argued that Russia had neither a past nor a future, and the reason for it was that Muscovy had received the light of Christianity not from Rome but from a corrupt and decaying Byzantium and, therefore, Russia had become not an integrated part of humanity but a "rump" of Western civilization. The only salvation for Russia was in a return to the true mother Church of the West, Rome. Nicholas issued an order pronouncing Chaadayev officially mad and had him put in an asylum.

Later on in 1845 the Petrashevsky Circle which had organized the Fourierist society, dedicated to utopian socialism, was cruelly suppressed by Nicholas. One of the leaders of this idealistic socialist movement was the literary critic Vissarion Bielinsky (1811-1848), who was to become a malicious opponent of Shevchenko, merged his opposition to autocracy with Russian imperialistic Messianism, proclaiming in 1840:

> We envy our grandsons and great-grandsons who are predestined in 1940 to witness Russia lead the civilized world, dictate laws on arts and sciences, and receive tributes of respect and worship from all civilized mankind.[5]

Thus, in summing up, the Russian resistance to absolutism was inadequate, but it did nevertheless include small circles of the rising intelligentsia.

On the other hand, Russian absolutism received inside the empire strong ideological support from the mystical and Messianistic Slavophils who believed that the Russian Orthodox church, the Russian village commune, and Russian autocracy were meant to save Russia from European decay and disintegration. The Slavophils presented their concept of Russia's destiny as a model for the whole of humanity, especially for Western Europe.

Later on, the political philosophy of Slavophilism was partly merged with Panslavism. This merger deeply stimulated the aggressive Russian imperialism and chauvinism. It also unleashed again the old still potent force of the legend that "Moscow was the Third Rome," an idea once proclaiming Moscow as the only depository of true Christianity and the Muscovites as a chosen people. A literary giant like Dostoyevsky, once a member of the Petrashevsky Circle, even became later the herald of ideological Russian autocracy, imperialism, anti-Catholicism, and anti-Semitism.

What little intellectual atmosphere there was in the Russian Empire during Nicholas I's rule, during which nearly the whole span of Shevchenko's life was cast, can easily be grasped from the following quotes taken from the works of the celebrated Russian lyric poet, Fjodor Tyutchev (1807-1873) who wrote also a special poem to justify Russia's cruel suppression of the Polish Revolution of 1830-31. . . .

A contemporary of Shevchenko, Tyutchev maintained in the poem which he composed in 1848, "Russia and the Revolution," that between Russia and Western Europe "no treaties are possible between these two worlds" because "the existence of one alone is equivalent to the death of the other."[6] Tyutchev concluded his discussion with a prophecy that everything in the West would be destroyed by the Revolution: "The Europe of Charlemagne and the Europe of the 1815 Treaties, the Roman Papacy, and all Western Kingdoms, Catholic and Protestant . . ." after the death of Europe there will appear a "vaster Empire floating like a sacred ark. Then who will dare to doubt the Russian mission?"[7]

Tyutchev's chauvinism reached fantastic heights. Not only did he regard the uniting of the Slavs as Russia's duty toward her own destiny which was to form in the end a higher type of civilization, but he also expected Russia to conquer the entire world. These ideas are revealed in his well known poem "Russian Geography:"

Moscow, and the city of Peter and the city of Constantine—
These are the sacred capitals of Russian Tsardom . . .
But where is its end? And where are its borders
To the North, to the East, to the South, and toward sunset?
They will be revealed by the fates to future times . . .
Seven internal seas and seven great rivers . . .

From the Nile to the Neva, from the Elbe to China,
From the Volga to the Euphrates, from the Ganges to the
Danube . . .
This is Russian Tsardom . . . and it will not disappear with
the ages
As the Holy Spirit foresaw and Daniel foretold.[8]

Thus the Russian Metternichism of Tsar Nicholas I did have the strong emotional support of some Russian chauvinist circles which made it possible for him with the help of the dreaded "Third Division" of His Majesty's personal Chancellery (founded in 1826) to terrorize and muzzle the country. It was not the first nor the last time that an omnipotent political intelligence service coupled with a well-controlled corps of gendarmes were used for this miserable purpose.

Now that we have surveyed the main characteristics of this dark age of the reign of Tsar Nicholas I we can look to the father of modern Russian history, Nicholas Karamzin (1766-1826) for a clue to understanding it. "Uncivilized peoples love liberty; civilized peoples love order, and there can be no order without autocracy," Karamzin wrote. "Autocracy is the soul, the life of Russia."

### *Shevchenko — Europe's Freedom Fighter*

THERE have been two Ukrainian writers who, although they used different weapons, have denounced Russian autocracy. The first was Mykola Hohol (Russian Gogol), the author of *Taras Bulba*. Hohol used satire and was aware that from all the sublime pinnacle of Tsarist absolutism, with all its colorful uniforms and decorations, to the ridiculous was but a mere step, and so he created in 1836 his "Inspector General." The laughter Hohol provoked continued to the time of the Revolution in the Russian Empire. But even Hohol later broke down under the influence of Russian mysticism.

The second one from Ukraine to denounce Russian autocracy was Taras Shevchenko. It was at the apogee of Russian absolutism that Shevchenko began to defend the human rights of peasants bound in serfdom by putting forward in the name of Christ the ideas of social justice and national liberation. With his deep emotion-packed poems he became a fanatical fighter against divine right-absolutism, against serfdom, a hell-on-earth kind of life with its cruel exploitation of the masses, with its bottomless depravity, immorality toward women, and bestiality toward children. Above all, Shevchenko became a fighter against Russian imperialism and colonialism, proclaiming "holy liberty" as the highest value of life. Therefore, he cursed Chmelnicky and glorified Mazepa for his uncompromising fight against Russia.

Shevchenko defended the liberty not only of the people of Ukraine but of all nations enslaved by Russia, from Finland to Rumania, from Poland to the Caucasus and Turkestan, including also the persecuted Jews. It is not widely known that under the public declaration of leading writers and scholars in the Russian Empire who supported the demand for equalization of civil rights for Jews in the Empire is also the signature of T. Shevchenko, together with the signatures of the distinguished Ukrainian writers Marko Vovchok and P. Kulish, in company with Russian writers like I. Turgenev, N. Nekrasov, S. Aksakov, P. Melnikov, N. Chernyshevsky, and others.[9]

Shevchenko united the Ukrainian national movement with the Western European camp of progress, democracy, and humanity, and he integrated it as well into the common struggle of European culture against Russian Tsarism, absolutism, imperialism, and genocide. In that dark age of absolutism in Russia, Shevchenko unfurled in one of his poems the flag of American republicanism, proclaiming as the ideal of Ukraine: "The new and just law of George Washington" and dedicated his nation to the ideals of the American Declaration of Independence of 1776. In his "Testament," which is the second anthem of the Ukrainians, he commanded them to rise and to break the Russian chains.

Shevchenko's world outlook is free from chauvinism; he embraces all peoples, and all mankind. Above all, he was a pious Christian. Therefore, he held in deepest contempt the Russian official Orthodox church which supported Russian absolutism

Bust of T. Shevchenko as a guide of the Ukrainian Nation (with beard after his exile) by Alexander Archipenko. Detroit City Museum of Fine Arts.

and imperialism. Shevchenko was a keen reader of the Bible and for him to be a poet meant to be an apostle of truth, freedom, and mercy—it meant being a messenger of the everlasting God Who is love and Who brings love to all mankind.

Thus Shevchenko shaped and formed the Ukrainian national ideal and the contemporary Ukrainian nationalism to socially and politically liberating forces. In addition, he inseparably united these with the ideals of Western Europe, but especially with those of the Founding Fathers of the United States of America.

Shevchenko's weapons against Tsar Nicholas' absolutism,

therefore, were the Gospel of true Christianity, which meant: freedom, justice mercy and charity—and the ideas of the American Declaration of Independence.

When and how did Shevchenko meet with these American ideas and America which was separated from Ukraine and Ukrainians not only by the ocean but by the Iron Curtain of Russian absolutism with its censorship and its "Third Division" of Tsar Nicholas? What significance have these meetings of Shevchenko with America for contemporary history being made every day behind the Russian Communist Iron Curtain with its still present censorship and "Third Division" police force now modernized but nevertheless in existence to perpetuate Soviet absolutism?

## II

### *Shevchenko Meets America*

JUST at the very apex of the power of Russian absolutism and imperialism which occurred during the reign of Nicholas I, Providence saw fit to give to Ukraine and to all the victims of Russian imperialism this poet Taras Shevchenko. In his short life of 47 years Shevchenko came in contact with America at least four times and was exposed through these contacts to basic American political thought and to key American personalities.

The first opportunity he had to become acquainted with America was through the writings of the American novelist Washington Irving (1783-1859). He had read the biography of Christopher Columbus, the discoverer of the American continent, in a Russian translation.[10]

Was the reading of this book simply an accident or was it generated by a special interest in America, provoked by some discussions about "the land of freedom" with his teacher Bryulov or some friends? Anyway the seed for Shevchenko's interest in America was planted surely to grow. . . .

The second time Shevchenko mentioned America was in the year 1857. After the New Tsar, Alexander II, granted him amnesty from his life sentence to serve "as a private in the military

Courtesy of the Collection of American Literature in the Yale University Library.

Washington Irving (1783-1859)

barracks" in the Asiatic borderlands, Shevchenko was returning to St. Petersburg when he saw his first steamship on the Volga river. He definitely did know that it was an invention by the American Robert Fulton, and he prophetically welcomed this invention as a signal of the dawn of the industrial and political revolutions not only in Russia but in the entire world. He wrote thus in his diary:

> Great Fulton! Great Watt! Your young child which is growing not by the day but by the hour will soon devour the whips, thrones, and crowns, and have the diplomats and landlords for dessert, playing with them like a child with a gumdrop. What the Encyclopaedists began in France will be fulfilled all over our planet by your child of tremendous genius. My prophecy is certain.

Self Portrait of Robert Fulton.

What is remarkable in this commentary is not only Shevchenko's anticipation of the industrial and political revolution in the Russian Empire and in the entire world but his awareness also of the origins of this revolution and his knowledge of and acquaintance with the ideas of the French Encyclopaedists which were eventually to find their expression in the American Revolution.

As we can see, Shevchenko possessed a keen historical perspective which provided him with unusual insight into the future just as it had prepared him for the moving experience of seeing

FULTON'S HISTORY-MAKING STEAMBOAT PASSING WEST POINT
Drawn from life by St. Memin

his first Fulton steamboat on the Volga. This historical perspective also granted Shevchenko a deep understanding of East European history.

Returning from exile Shevchenko passed a night in Astrachan and was overcharged for his room. In his diary (August 10, 1857) he complained and compared the price to prices in "San Francisco." Apparently Shevchenko read some descriptions of the contemporary U.S.A. or some friends informed him about life in America.

The third time Shevchenko had personal contact with America was through the great Negro American actor, Ira Aldridge (1807-1867) who merited inclusion in the *Encyclopedia Americana*.

Who was Ira Aldridge?[11] He was the grandson of a Senegal tribal chieftain who had been slain by his tribesmen because he had ruled that prisoners of war should be exchanged and not sold into slavery. His only remaining son, Ira's father, was rescued by an American missionary, brought to America, converted to Christianity, and became a minister of a Negro congregation

Ira Aldridge as Othello.

in New York where Ira was born. Of course, it was the wish of his father for Ira also to become a minister, but Ira's desire was to act.

One can easily imagine the social status of an Afro-American in the United States at that time. Ira could only join an amateur group, but he found his way to Edmund Kean, the noted English actor who visited America for a guest performance. Kean liked the talented aspiring actor and took him along to London. In 1826 Aldridge made his debut as Othello in the Shakespearean tragedy at the Royalty theater there, and his first performance made him a famous actor.

Ira returned to America, but was not accepted by the theatrical profession, so he left America never to return. He travelled all over Europe, appearing as guest actor in many of Shakespeare's plays, being decorated by European kings and emperors, arriving finally in 1858 at the capital of the Russian Tsars, St. Petersburg.

One of the great salons in what was then St. Petersburg was the palace of Count and Countess Fjodor Tolstoy[12] which was a center of the social and intellectual life frequented by writers, artists, actors, and liberal aristocrats. Count Tolstoy was the Vice President of the Imperial Academy of Fine Arts, and he was, in fact, the man whose influences in the court and on the new Tsar Alexander achieved the amnesty for Shevchenko. In St. Petersburg Shevchenko was a daily guest of the Tolstoys, and on

Count Fjodor Tolstoy, a Portrait Drawn with Black and White pencils by T. Shevchenko.

December 30, 1859 Countess Tolstoy asked him to come in the evening for a special recital. "Please, Taras Gregorovich, come between 7 and 10 p.m. Ira Aldridge is going to recite from Shakespeare."

Shevchenko died in the year 1861. Aldridge died six years later in 1867 during a second Russian tour and was buried in Lodz, Poland, near Warsaw. Aldridge was given a state funeral.

For Shevchenko, who was well acquainted by Russian translations with the works of Shakespeare, Byron, Dickens, and Scott, Aldridge became the phonetical herald of the Anglo-American living sounds—both words and language—and a living part of America where the Negroes had a fate similar to that of the Ukrainian peasants in Russia.

Mrs. Marie Trommer-Trembicka[13] published a fine article in 1939 which began:

> It was undoubtedly the power of destiny that brought and drew together the two flaming kindred souls, the two persecuted slaves from countries far apart, who succeeded in escaping from brutality of their environment into humane, cultural worlds.

Mrs. Trommer-Trembicka gives us a good summary of the friendship that existed between Aldridge and Shevchenko using contemporary materials:

> Shevchenko came at the appointed time to the Tolstoys, saw and heard Ira Aldridge, and was deeply impressed by Aldridge's genius. That very evening found the two men sitting in a corner sofa in a fond embrace. They could not understand each other's language, but their interest and attachment to one another was immediate. With the assistance of Tolstoy's daughter who served as interpreter they succeeded in expressing their thought. They began to meet regularly. Shevchenko used to come in early. He was engaged in drawing a portrait of Aldridge, and while waiting would sharpen his pencils and arrange the lighting effects. Aldridge was always late. He would rush in, take off his cloak, and inquire: "Is the artist here?" Shevchenko, impatient to see his model, used to reprimand him for being late. Feeling guilty, Aldridge would assume the required pose without any comment. He could not keep his pose very long though.

Aldridge would begin to fidget and grimace and Shevchenko would swear good-naturedly in the Ukrainian language: "Oh, you child of the devil!"

Aldridge, seeing his friend's displeasure, would jump up and begin to chant Negro slave songs, to dance Negro dances, and to present scenes from his beloved Shakespeare. Shevchenko would leave his drawing board and join in the chanting. Then both would dance. Suddenly they would kiss and cry. Long quiet conversations would take place between them. They used to speak about the similarity of their fate.

Aldridge spoke about the Negro slavery and Shevchenko about the peasants in Russia. They spoke of the large sums of money Aldridge was sending to America to allevi-

Ira Aldridge, a Portrait Drawn with Black and White Pencils by T. Shevchenko.

ate the suffering of his brethren, and Shevchenko told of doing his bit by giving to the Ukrainian serfs as much as he could spare from his small earnings as a poet.

They spoke of the heartaches they had lived through, shared their bitter persecutions. The songs they sang were echoes of the honest, pure souls striving for the liberation of their people.

Aldridge would often visit Shevchenko in his furnished room. The poet usually kept his room in great disorder, but when he expected his friend, he would clean it thoroughly. The two would lock themselves in for hours, talking and singing. At other times they would be joined by the artist Mikeshin. Aldridge, enchanted by Russian and especially Ukrainian melodies, used to participate in the singing. Later, he would burst into singing poetical English romances still unknown in Eastern Europe.

Shevchenko working constantly at his portrait of Aldridge would drop his pencil and listen. Regardless of these musical sittings, Shevchenko succeeded in completing his friend's portrait eventually. Often, after his glamorous performances of *Othello,* Aldridge would appear in the Tolstoy's drawing room seeking the company of Shevchenko. The poet, imbued with enthusiasm, would praise the acting of Aldridge who spoke his lines in English with the supporting roles being spoken in German. Shevchenko used to be displeased though, with the fact that the Russian actors' playing with Aldridge did not come up to the tragedian's standards. He disliked particularly the actress who played Desdemona, and would say to Aldridge: "Why didn't you strangle her in the very first act?"

Besides his part in *Othello,* the American actor also played King Lear using white make-up for the part. His acting, remarkable in all respects, brought Shevchenko to a great emotional frenzy. . . .

On February 28, 1861, the two friends parted forever. For Shevchenko died on that day, his health having been undermined by lifelong privations. He was buried in Ukraine on a hill above the Dnieper river.

Once, in June, 1861, Ira Aldridge completed his engagement in St. Petersburg and was decorated by Tsar Alexander II with the Russian Cross. Then, carrying with him numberless gifts presented to him by admirers and by

> aristocratic ladies of the capital, he left on a tour of the Russian Empire. His itinerary took him to Ukraine, to the country that Shevchenko had cried and sang about. And, Aldridge wept over the grave of his friend, the grave which towered on the hill above the Dnieper.
>
> Ira Aldridge lived six years longer than Shevchenko. He died while on his second Russian tour of 1867. He was accorded a state funeral and his numerous decorations glittering with gold and precious stones were carried on a cushion. He was mourned by the populace and by the highest officials of the town, who walked behind the bier.
>
> Ira Aldridge died knowing that his dream of freedom for the Negro in America had become a fact, while Shevchenko on his day of death, was unaware that the Russian peasants were to be set free under the Imperial Decree which was issued in St. Petersburg on March 5. He did die happy though with the realization that through his financial help his relatives were no longer among the serfs. He had succeeded in winning their release by great effort just a few months before the slavery abolition decree was made known.

The Russian Communist *Agitprop* specialists (Department of Agitation and Propaganda of the Russian Communist party) did not overlook this topic, which connected Shevchenko with Aldridge, Ukraine with America, and the Negro problem inside present day America. *Literaturna Gazeta,* the organ of the Union of Writers of Ukraine, in its April 7, 1961 issue published the information that:

> The English film producer Herbert Marshall was just shooting a movie on the life of the great Negro actor, Ira Aldridge. The script is written by Marshall himself together with the Soviet writer Leonid Rakhmanov. The movie is based on the friendship between Aldridge and Shevchenko and Shevchenko's friend, the actor Shchepkin. The leading part will be played by Paul Robeson.[14]

Apparently the film is still not realized. But we can learn from an interview of O. Novycky with Herbert Marshall entitled, "Herbert Marshall: 'I Love Shevchenko'" in *Literaturna Ukraina,* October 25, 1963 that Marshall is writing a book on Ira Aldridge and especially one topic interests him:

> Shevchenko and Aldridge. I love Shevchenko very much, he stated . . . especially since I learned so much about him on my trip to Kaniw where Shevchenko is buried. I became deeply persuaded that Shevchenko was truly a folk bard who is really loved and respected by the common people.
>
> The mentioned work of Marshall on Ira Aldridge is of great interest also for the Ukrainian reader, since it discussed the encounter and friendship of the sons of two nations, both of whom experienced brutal oppression. With great cordiality the Ukrainian society welcomed Aldridge who in these far years brought the immortal Shakespearean image to the Ukrainian onlookers in Kiev, Odessa, Zhytomyr, and also to Jelysawetohrad, where the unsurpassable acting of the great tragedian saw also the master of the Ukrainian theater, Ivan Tobilevich (Karpenko-Karyj).
>
> Marshall fundamentally analyzed the life and activity of Aldridge and his gigantic work for the recreation of Shakespearean personages . . . Aldridge carried Ukraine in his heart. Twice he visited us. Ukraine gave him such a friend as Shevchenko. Ira was enchanted by Shevchenko, his people, nature, music, songs . . . And this love is transferred now to Marshall . . . Soon he will again visit us in order to continue his work on the book about Aldridge, preparing it for an Ukrainian edition and also in order to write the script for an artistic movie about the cordial friendship between Shevchenko and Aldridge.

In summing up, let us say that the information published in *Literaturna Gazeta* in 1961 was rather premature since the script for the film is still not written. But a book will soon appear and Marshall, an old friend of Russian Communism, has done research among the English translators of Shevchenko and has himself translated a series of his poems.

The fourth and most important time in which Shevchenko came in contact with America and the spirit of her Founding Fathers was when reading the American Declaration of Independence of 1776. The strong influence that this document had on Shevchenko is reflected in his emotion-packed reaction which produced his revolutionary political program in which he advocated the adoption of the ideals of the Founding Fathers of America for his own oppressed Ukraine:

When will our waiting for Washington with the new and just law be at last fulfilled? He will come someday in spite of all obstacles!

IN CONGRESS, JULY 4, 1776.

The unanimous Declaration of the thirteen united States of America,

The upperpart of the American Declaration of Independence.

Obviously, Shevchenko was convinced of the decisive importance of that memorable document of the American Founding Fathers in the struggle for moral order in the world. These ideas of the American Declaration represented for him the climax of mankind's battle for freedom; these American ideas represented to him the very antithesis of the Russian Empire of Nicholas I with its official ideology of imposed uniformity, Russian absolutism, Russian Orthodoxy, Russian nationalism-chauvinism, and its accompanying evil, serfdom.

These lines of Shevchenko about Washington were and still are presently much discussed among historians and Shevchenkologists inside and outside the Soviet Union. They pose some questions, which demand clarification. Recently in the free world these problems were discussed by Bohdan Krawciw who wrote an article "When Will Our Waiting for Washington Be Fulfilled?—a Genesis of Shevchenko's Just and New Law."[15]

(a) The first problem is when and where did Shevchenko get acquainted with Washington's name and the text of our Declaration of Independence. What nationality, or rather what nation's intellectual elite mediated in that case? How did the contagion of America's ideals infect Shevchenko?

(1) In the Soviet Union the official Communist party interpretation requires one to interpret these lines of Shevchenko as

the "noble" influence of the Russians and of Russian literature on him. They must be explained as "the result of the activity and struggle of the revolutionary Russian democracy headed by such men as Herzen, Bielinsky, Dobroliubov, and Chernyshevsky."

All of this, of course, only reasserts that the Russians are the fountainhead of all democratic ideas for Shevchenko and Ukraine. The facts are that Dobroliubov and Chernyshevsky were still teenagers as Shevchenko wrote his revolutionary poems. In the publications of Herzen, one will look in vain for an enthusiasm for the ideas of the American Declaration of Independence and George Washington.

(2) Bohdan Krawciw supports the explanation given by W. Porsky in his "Shevchenko and Washington."[16] Porsky called attention to the great popularity of the American War of Independence and of Washington, the man, among the Polish gentry families on the right bank of the Dnieper in Ukraine at the beginning of the nineteenth century and wrote:

> A quarter century later, when the Ukrainian Decabrists (Decembrists) prepared their rebellion, in the Kiev province, Washington and the political regime in office in the United States were for the Ukrainians the ideal of a national hero and a national program of action. The pattern of the American regime in some parts and ideas went into the project of state reforms which were discussed in the circles of the Southern Decabrists. The reverence for the "Father of the Fatherland," as Washington was called in America, is confirmed by memoirs.

To prove that a cult of Washington did exist at that time in Ukraine, Porsky cited the Diary of Mr. P. Rosciszewska from the Kievan province:

> May 21, 1827—I also visited the Trzeciak family in Jaropovci. What a beautiful garden they have! Trees, flowers, and a beautiful setting. Mrs. Trzeciak showed me Washington's beloved tree—the *Bignonia Catalpa*. The hapless Muravjov always used to take off his hat before the tree saying, that one must pay homage to the tree of the great man . . . Alas, a few steps away grow tall cypresses and frowning pines, and they remind one of this splendid young

man and of his unhappy fate. Together with Mrs. Trzeciak we wept there, moved by remembrance of him and by our grief. . . .[17]

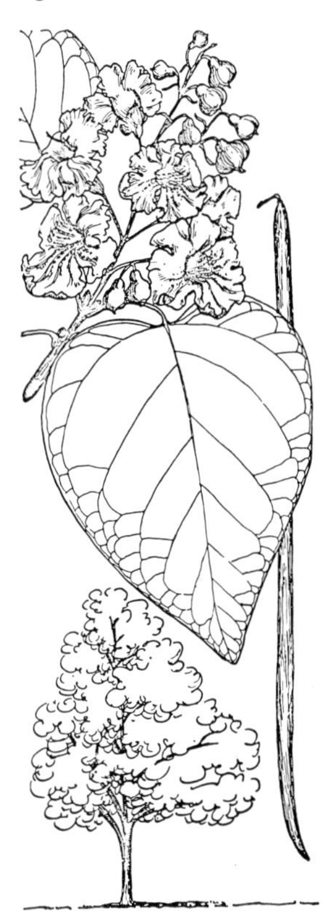

**Catalpa bignonioides**

*Catal´pa bignonioi´des*
*(Macrocatalpa; C. syringaefolia)*

Cigar Tree; Common Catalpa;
Indian-Bean; Southern Catalpa

Southeastern United States

Porsky saw a continuity of American and Washington traditions in the secret organization which emerged 20 years later in Kiev, the Cyrilo-Methodian Brotherhood. Shevchenko was associated with this group which began in the closing months of 1845. The Brotherhood propagated the idea of a federation for all Slavic nationalities according to the pattern of the United States of America. (This fact recognized also the Communist I. Pilhuk, "Kyrylo-Mefodijivske Bratstvo" . . . Vitchyzna (1946) pp. 189-200.) In this way the name of George Washington again became a banner. One member of the Brotherhood, Juriy Andruzky, after being captured by spies for Tsar Nicholas, confessed that all the brothers were united by the idea of a federation of all Slavic nationalities according to the model given by the U.S.A. or that offered by the French Constitution. The special secret aim espoused by this Ukrainian Brotherhood was the reestablishment of the independent Ukrainian Hetman State although its declared intention was to organize a Ukrainian state inside the planned Slavic federation.

In evaluating these facts—(1) of the popularity of the American fight for independence and its hero and leader, George Washington, in Ukraine in the first decades of the nineteenth century, (2) the report of the member of the Cyrilo-Methodian Brotherhood, Jurij Andruzky, about its ideas and aims,—Porsky and Krawciw regard them as the original sources for Shevchenko's longing for the coming of "Washington's just and new law."

Actually it was this longing and hope for the victorious penetration of the American ideas into the Slavic world that kept the Ukrainian intellectual elite alive during this trying period and which was as well the root of the now famous programmatic exclamation of Shevchenko. Thus, according to this explanation, the geographical locale of the genesis of Shevchenko's philosophy is Ukraine although the national roots are partly Ukrainian and partly Polish.

(3) There is also the possibility of a third interpretation of the genesis of Shevchenko's philosophy which gives more stress to Polish influences on him. In St. Petersburg Shevchenko had a roommate, a Polish revolutionary named Leonard Demski, who acquainted him with the works of Adam Mickiewicz and of the historian Lelewel. This was in 1838. Between the formation of the Cyrilo-Methodian Brotherhood in Kiev (1845-46) and the writing by Shevchenko of the "Jurodywyj (The Mad Tsar)" in the year 1857, which is the work containing the "Washington exclamation," Shevchenko was in exile in the Asiatic borderlands. When he arrived in Orenburg where more than 2,000 Poles were also in political exile, the Poles welcomed him. A banquet was even prepared for him by these men with the leadership of the Polish poet who was to be Shevchenko's lifelong friend, Bronislaw

Zaleski. Another of the prominent Polish exiles, Edward Zheligowski, was also a friend to Shevchenko and dedicated a poem to him entitled, "To Brother Taras Shevchenko." But the factor of the greatest importance was, in our opinion, Shevchenko's friendship and correspondence with Zygmunt Sierakowski,[18] one of the leaders of the Polish Revolution against Russia in 1863.

All these Polish revolutionaries and exiles were deeply conscious of the fact that they continued the mission of Kosciuszko and of Pulaski. And here it is well to recall that Pulaski was the leader of the anti-Russian Bar Confederation. (Bar is a city in Ukraine.) Kosciuszko and Pulaski had participated in the American War of Independence and their names were closely linked with the name of George Washington. It is impossible to imagine that these Poles whom Shevchenko had known since 1838 did not discuss with him on many occasions the fate of Poland as compared to the fate of free America. Shevchenko even dedicated a poem to these Polish patriots, and he regarded the fall of Poland as a catastrophe to Ukraine as well. It may be that just this very American-Polish ideological climate contributed significantly to the genesis of the Shevchenko pronouncement about Washington.

(4) Finally, Professor Clarence Manning, of Columbia university, suspects a fourth interpretation, a view which has its merits. The American writer Washington Irving (1783-1859) visited England from 1815-1832 and became friends with several Russian diplomats who made his work known in the Pushkin Circle in St. Petersburg. Shevchenko mentioned in his *Artist* which was written in 1856 that while under the influence of his teacher Bryulov he had previously read Irving's *Biography of Columbus*. In 1855-59 Irving published his *Life of Washington* which was certainly known among the circles Shevchenko frequented, especially to his friends the Tolstoys where he also would have become acquainted with the work. In a letter to me of April 10, 1961 Professor Manning wrote:

> It is undoubtedly through some translation of Irving around 1857 that Shevchenko received the inspiration of Washington, or else it came from Polish circles interested in the rela-

tions of Washington and Kosciusko. I am sure that Dobroliubov and his group were not involved in it at all.

Finally, let me make the following remarks:

First, it is really amazing how through so many channels the American ideas radiated into the absolutist Russian Empire and how deep was the veneration for George Washington in spite of all the censorship enforced in Poland and Ukraine.

Secondly, I am inclined to accept as the genesis of Shevchenko's programmatic pronouncement demanding a Washington and the enactment of his ideals for Ukraine the principle of manifold sources while arranging several sources in the following order of importance: Ukrainian, Polish, and finally, perhaps English-American.

In keeping with the mentioned Russian position, Krawciw also has checked Herzen's *Collected Works* insofar as they appeared without support for the official Russian Communist thesis. But the official Soviet Russian Shevchenkologists would not admit the existence of the above mentioned facts, of course.

Therefore, the Russian theory of the genesis of Shevchenko's thought is falsified as to the "influence of the Russian revolutionary democrats" since in these presented facts, inevitably and systematically omitted by the Russians, are to be found the basic American ideas of revolutionary self-determination of the people which are obviously dangerous to present day Soviet Russian imperialism and colonialism, just as they once were for the old Tsarist Russia.

(b) The second problem connected with Shevchenko's allusion to Washington is the question of understanding its significance. The interpretation of scholars before World War I and of those historians and Shevchenkologists who have since 1918 come to the free world is unanimous:

1) Washington was the victorious leader of the American Revolution against British imperialism and his victories brought realization of the principles of the American Declaration of Independence and helped establish the United States as a nation.

2) Consequently, Shevchenko expected a Ukrainian Washington to lead the Ukrainian revolution against Russian Tsarist

imperialism and to establish a Ukrainian independent state as a republic on the basis of the ideas of the American Declaration of Independence.

3) Shevchenko by pronouncing a characteristically Washingtonian program of political action for the Ukraine shaped and formed Ukrainian nationalism. Therefore, for Ukrainians, in the political sense Shevchenko and Washington are inseparable. All native Ukrainians remembered Washington's ideals singing Shevchenko's "Testament" as a national anthem in the Russian Empire and do it even now in the Soviet Union.

4) Naturally, the Ukrainians claim Washingtonian revolutionary self-determination not only for themselves, but, in the spirit of Shevchenko's ideology, for all by the Russian-imperialists oppressed nationalities which means for all oppressed peoples from Finland to Rumania, from Poland to the Caucasus and Turkestan and also for the Jewish people. In short, Ukrainians claim the right of self-determination for all captive nations.

One can imagine what such an ideology did mean for old Tsarist Russian imperialism. One can understand what it means for contemporary Russian Soviet imperialism—the imperialism which has been identified by the distinguished Russian philosopher Nicholas Berdyaev[19] in a most authoritative way as the "third appearance of the old Muscovite imperialism."

Therefore, the Russian Communist dictatorship over the Liberal Arts and the Sciences, and which managed to subordinate to itself the Fine Arts and Literature as well, had to face this interpretation. It is certainly understandable that with the establishment in Russia of Communist totalitarianism the mere mention of the name of George Washington in Shevchenko's *Kobzar* evokes again and again such emotional outbursts as it does from inside the Kremlin.

It is true that Washington's name is still included in the editions of Shevchenko's work which were printed in the Soviet Union, and the reason behind this mildly surprising fact is that it simply could not be erased. The sentence of *Kobzar* in which Shevchenko refers to Washington became a most quoted saying in Ukrainian, one which everyone knew and knows by heart.

But in compliance with the directives of the Russian Communist party, Washington's name is played down through the use of different methods which vary from the exercise of reprisals against the editors of Shevchenko's works to the elimination of footnotes referring to the Washington passage. There has been, too, a systematical discreditation of Washington as the leader of the American War of Independence.

As we can see, Washington became a "controversial" personality for the Russian Communists especially because of Shevchenko's use of his name in his programmatic statement. He was all the more so since, according to all recollections published about the revolution in the Russian Empire in 1917, the revolutionary banner against the Russian Empire of the Tsars was just this: Taras Shevchenko. The report of a noted literary critic and leader of the Ukrainian Socialist Federalist party, Andrij Nikowsky, about the developments of this era is characteristic in its findings:

> Over all the flags, music bands, machine guns, manifestations, Hetmans, politicians, parties, leaders, and parliaments there ruled and dominated alone the Ukrainian poet. Monarchist Russia, the ideologists of centralization, and the parochial pedants were forced to bow their heads before him, the great and invincible master of the rusty pen. The victory was with you, Poet! The victorious Ukrainian revolution was carried out not by a general, a hero, a Tsar, a diplomat, or a German school teacher, but by a poet.[20]

Nikowsky is right when he says "by a poet," but a poet with a political program that could be expressed in one word: Washington. All the revolutionary processions in the cities of Ukraine, even in St. Petersburg and Moscow, were led by portraits or lithographs of Shevchenko flanked by the Ukrainian national banners. I recently prepared a description of this era of Eastern European history[21] part of which reads:

> The ideas of the American Declaration of Independence represented by Taras Shevchenko's work and life blew to pieces the Russian Empire, the prison of nations. This was simply a continuation of the American Revolution in Eastern Europe. Tragically, America then, not grasping the meaning of

these events, decidedly contributed to the rise of and rebuilding of the new Russian Empire. . . .

Therefore, the hatred felt by the Russian Communists for Shevchenko was fanatical. In 1918 a part of Ukraine was occupied by Red troops when another example of Shevchenko's enormous influence on his people was compiled by V. Vynnychenko.[22] Vynnychenko reported that pictures of Shevchenko were frequently torn down from the walls of houses and trampled on by the commissars on their searches.

Only later, after the full establishment of the Communist dictatorship over Ukraine, was Shevchenko "re-instated" as the bard of Ukraine in order not to provoke any further anti-Russian nationalism among the Ukrainian masses by a continued persecution of the poet. During the New Economic Policy period (NEP) which continued to 1929, the Communist party ordered the creation of a new image of Shevchenko which would project him as a "Christ of Socialism."[23] Koriak, the writer, even had to proclaim him as "one of the first poet-prophets of the proletariat and of the great social revolution of the future.[24] A good survey of all of the images of Shevchenko that were the products of Communist inspiration has been done by Petro Odarchenko,[25] an exiled Soviet scholar. The study also does a good job of presenting the later phases of official Soviet treatment of Shevchenko.

Soon after the liquidation of the NEP (1930-33) by the Russian Communist regime, one of the most noxious acts of this new policy was the show trial of the "Union for the Liberation of Ukraine," in which the chief defendant was Serhij Jefremov, the editor of Taras Shevchenko's *Collected Works* and a member of the Ukrainian Academy of Sciences in Kiev. There also followed the systematic destruction of Shevchenko scholarship by the regime. This Russian Communist reaction was unavoidable and even to be expected because along with the Washington political program Shevchenko's work also includes an interpretation of Ukraine's history that was wholely unpalatable to the Communists: A condemnation of Hetman Bohdan Chmelnicky who was responsible for the commitment of Ukraine to the alliance with the Tsar of Muscovy in 1654 at Perejaslaw. In it there was as well a glorification of Hetman Ivan Mazepa who had attempted to regain Ukrainian freedom and statehood through an alliance with Charles XII of Sweden.

It is remarkable that in spite of all the Russian Communist persecutions of independent scholarship and thinking there could still appear at that time such a publication as that of the foremost Marxist Shevchenkologist, Andrij Richycky which contained the following formulation of Shevchenko's political ideology:[26]

> Shevchenko's views of the national problem could, in Richysky's opinion, be best described as "an ideology of revolutionary national liberation." Shevchenko, as Richycky maintained, hated Tsar Peter I and Tsarina Catherine II as well as the Ukrainian Hetman Bohdan Chmelnicky, who "betrayed the revolution and went to Perejaslav to swear allegiance to Moscow." Shevchenko led the fight against the foreign domination of his land and hated Peter I for defeating Mazepa at Poltava. "Shevchenko," wrote Richycky, "posed the problem of a united national front and the revolutionary struggle of the bourgeoisie for a national state—the problem of a national, bourgeois and democratic revolution." Finally, Richycky held that Shevchenko sought a modern form for his ideas of nationality and his ideas of the national state of the future when he wrote: "When shall we get our Washington with a new and just law? One day we shall."

Shevchenkologist Richycky also said himself:

> Here the author, Shevchenko, has in mind nothing less than his people's struggle for their liberation from a foreign yoke and the creation of a Ukrainian state, namely a republic. Here in the image of Washington with a new and just law, in the image of the national and military leader of the American bourgeoisie in its war of liberation against England, and in the image of the first president of the North American Republic Shevchenko expressed his program for a revolutionary war for independence of Ukraine as a republic.

Richycky was executed in 1933.

Washington continued to trouble the Russian Communists until V. Bojko found a "formula" with a reference to Lenin's theory of "two ways of capitalist development," which he applied to Shevchenko. According to Lenin, there were two kinds of capitalist evolution open to Russia, the Prussian or the American. Consequently, Bojko concluded, that, if Shevchenko would have been born a landowner, he would have chosen the Prussian type. But, being born a serf as he was and a peasant and so necessarily being against large estates, Shevchenko went the American way. Thus, also other Soviet commissars of literature rehabilitated Shevchenko and his works as "an objective expression of the struggle for the American path of development of capitalism in Russia.[27]

By 1934 Shevchenko studies were put under the direct control of the Russian Communist party, and this powerful organization was responsible for the publication of the official interpretation of Shevchenko under the title, "Theses of the Section on Culture and Propaganda of Leninism of the Central Committee of the Communist Party (Bolsheviks) of Ukraine on the Occasion of the 120th anniversary of the birthday of T. H. Shevchenko."

The new Party authority on Shevchenko was J. Shablovsky, who rewrote his book on Shevchenko in 1935 under the new title, "T. H. Shevchenko, His Life and Works." This time Shevchenko was interpreted as "the bourgeois representative of the revolutionary bourgeois peasant democracy," who expressed "the American path of bourgeois development." Thus the Russian Communists hoped by emphasizing the "American path" to falsify the true content of Shevchenko's Washingtonian program.

Since 1939, however, the falsification of Shevchenko by the Communist party "experts" has shifted into high gear, his reputation has been completely remade, his poems "re-interpreted," his biography "re-written" so that he became a "hero" and a vehicle for promoting Soviet patriotism and Russian nationalism.

For the present it is enough to quote only the contribution made at Moscow university by J. Dmyterko toward the falsification of Shevchenko's world outlook in his book, *Socio-Political and Philosophical Ideas of T. H. Shevchenko*.[28] In this work Shevchenko is presented as a "foster child" of the advanced Russian culture on whom "a beneficient influence" with regard to his world outlook "was also exercised by the advanced Russian natural sciences." According to Dmyterko, "The poet was organically tied to the Russian people with their advanced culture," and he "loved and fought for the union with the Russian people. . . ." This is the diabolical, up-side-down picture of Shevchenko that has been created by Russian Communist party directives in Moscow.

It is sufficient for our purposes here to provide only the conclusions of the present plight of Soviet Shevchenkology under Russian Communist dictatorship as it is reported by the noted authority, Petro Odarchenko:[29]

> Many important pronouncements by Shevchenko, especially those in favor of America, continue to be ignored by those two authors (Bilecky and Dejch). The entry from Shevchenko's diary in which he praises Fulton and Watt for their discoveries was omitted, as it was in a recent Soviet film on Shevchenko, where Fulton and Watt were replaced by "inventors." Shevchenko's dream of a Ukrainian Washington, in his poem "Jurodywyj" has also been forgotten. J. Iwakin, while discussing Shevchenko's "Jurodywyj," cites the well-known passage on Washington, although he describes the first president of the United States as "the leader of the revolutionary farmers' armies," the fighter for American independence from England is forgotten.

A similar fate has been dealt to the customary footnote commentary up to now included in the Soviet editions of Shevchenko's *Kobzar*. Bohdan Krawciw[30] gives a survey of all the twists and evasions contained in the Soviet editions. Another example of this manipulation is found in the work of the above mentioned Richycky who commented on the use of the name of Washington by Shevchenko in his "Jurodywyj:"

> Washington, first president of the U.S.A. Until the year 1783 North America belonged to England.

Richycky was subsequently accused of trying to suggest to readers that "Shevchenko fought for the separation of Ukraine from Russia just as Washington fought for the separation of the U.S.A. from Great Britain." This comment appeared in the "Kommunist" on April 11, 1934. Richycky, as was reported, was previously liquidated.

In 1939 the Academy edition of the *"Kobzar"* gave this footnote:

> George Washington—fighter for the liberation of North America from the rule of England in the second half of the eighteenth century. First president of the U.S.A.

In the 1950 edition of the *"Kobzar"* there is this comment:

> Washington—American statesman of the eighteenth century, great estate owner (landlord) who headed the struggle for independence from England. First president of the U.S.A. At the end of his activity he displayed an enmity towards the French Revolution and started to grant economic concessions to England.

Thus began the official line intended to create in Ukraine a "new image" of Washington as a "landlord" and, naturally, as an "exploiter," an "enemy of the revolution," an "unprincipled compromiser." Especially strong became this Communist directive even more so toward the end of the 1950's when the Cold War was nearing its climax.

In 1959 E. Kyryliuk in his monograph on Shevchenko wrote the following lines about Washington: "in his time (Shevchenko) could not universally grasp the activity of the distinguished bourgeois leader of the period of the struggle for independence from England." This attempt "to trim the stature of Washington" is continued in the Ukrainian Soviet Encyclopedia under the listing of "Washington," where Washington is presented as a person whose "peculiarities were a certain limitation of his political opinions and a conservatism which increased in his last years."

The most successful method used by the Russian Communist party in its plot to blot out the true interpretation of Shevchenko's passages on Washington is simply to pass over them in silence. Thus in the Shevchenko editions under the editorship of M. Rylsky for 1955, 1957, and 1959 any commentary about who Washington was is simply dropped. That is the case also in the *Kobzar* printed in 1961 published for "the toiling masses of Ukraine" in one hundred thousand copies. . . .

And yet, the "Washington-Shevchenko problem" is never bypassed by the ever-industrious Agitprop. Even while World War II damages were being surveyed, large masses of Ukrainian exiles reached Canada and the United States. Agitprop immediately began to scheme about how to get a foothold on the American continent for the distribution of the Russian Communist version of Shevchenko's place in history. Thus the "people of Ukraine" presented to the Canadian nation a monument of Shevchenko located in Palermo, Canada; it promptly became a propaganda center for the disbursement of Communist publications. Aroused, the Canadian Ukrainians took up the challenge and built their own monument to the true Shevchenko at Winnipeg, Man., Canada in 1961, unveiled by the then Prime Minister John J. Diefenbaker.

Soviet Moscow and the Ukrainian occupation regime became quite nervous when the Americans of Ukrainian descent next decided to answer their challenge with a monument in Washington, D.C., and when, not long afterward, the U.S. Congress accepted unanimously the Public Law 86-749 which was then signed by President Eisenhower authorizing the erection of a statue of Taras Shevchenko on public grounds in the nation's capital.

The whole Shevchenko-Washington ideological relationship and its symbolism have served to focus attention on this defensive action against the aggressive Agitprop actions here on the very American continent. How important this problem is to the Russian Communist party is well illustrated by the reaction in the Communist press against the projected monument in Washington.

In 1961 D. Ostrianyn wrote:[31]

> The Ukrainian bourgeois nationalists who are kept by the imperialists of the U.S.A. are trying to prove that Shevchenko allegedly wished to see a Ukraine on the pattern of the present U.S.A. To prove this, they cite his poem "Jurodywyj (The Madman)" in which the poet wrote:
>
> > When will we get our Washington with new and
> > righteous laws?
> > We surely will, some day.
>
> In these words Shevchenko contrasted the reactionary, rotten, autocratic order of serfdom with the political order defended by George Washington which was progressive in its

day. Today all the "righteous laws" in the U.S.A. have been buried; there exists a reign of the most high-handed reactionary social forces, ruthless enslavement of the workers, and racial and national discrimination. The American reactionaries and their hirelings, the Ukrainian bourgeois nationalists, will never succeed in turning the poet-revolutionary into a partisan of the American bourgeois order. It's no use. . . .

Leonid Novychenko also wrote in 1961:[32]

> Moreover, they (Ukrainian bourgeois nationalists) have gone so far as to try to represent Shevchenko as a propagator of the ill-famed "American way of life." Taking out of context a few lines about George Washington from the poem "The Feeble Minded," the Nationalist "experts on Shevchenko" are trying to prove that the poet "dreamt about Ukraine as a replica of the democratic United States. . . ."
>
> There are some lines in the poems of *Kobzar* which are now the subject of particularly "profound" and tendencious interpretation on the part of some overseas commentators. This is the well-known passage from "Jurodywyj (The Madman)":
>
> When will we get our Washington with new and
> righteous laws?
> We surely will, some day.
>
> Under conditions of feudal-serfdom reality, Shevchenko was paying his tribute with these words to the American bourgeois revolution of 1776, which the classicists of Marxist-Leninism consider as one of the great, truly liberating and truly revolutionary wars of that era.
>
> There is all reason to believe that by the phrase "new and righteous laws" and its association with the name of Washington, the poet had in mind, primarily, the excellent Declaration of Independence—the most important social-political document of that Revolution, which had become widely known to its contemporaries and their successors all over the world. The favorable attitude of the poet to these "laws" can be well understood only in connection with the concrete historical conditions of that time. . . .
>
> This is what Shevchenko valued highly in the ideological heritage of the American Revolution and in the activities

> of its leaders. He regarded them, like he regarded the French Eycyclopaedists and his close friends, the Russian Decembrists, as the precursors of the new revolutionary generation of which he was a part. But, it is a distortion of the historical truth to see in these words cited from "Jurodywyj" some kind of an orientation of the poet to his contemporary, and even less so to our contemporary version of an American bourgeois democracy. . . .

From silencing of any comments about Washington to making the above commentary (published, of course, with the approval of the Russian Communist commissars for Ukrainian literature) is a long way to come. And yet how far away is this official Communist interpretation from *the true meaning* of Taras Shevchenko's life and work! How far away from Shevchenko's feeling for Washington as well is this official Communist interpretation. And yet even the Marxist Richycky once fully understood Shevchenko although all he got for his scholarly honesty was to be shot. . . .

(c) And a third problem deserves mention here. Why does Shevchenko call the American Declaration of Independence "Washington's new and just law?" Surely he knew who drafted it. Of course, it can be easily explained by association of Washington's name with the document.

But I think the cause lies deeper than this. Shevchenko as a revolutionary had the deepest respect, first of all, not for the "drafters" of the Declaration but for those who made its realization possible through hard fought battles and final victory. He had reverence for the men who risked their own lives in the name of the "new and just law," in the name of a cause in which he also believed. For Shevchenko, General Washington was a victorious American Mazepa.

In Shevchenko's mind, therefore, it was not those who wrote the Declaration of Independence who were the heroes but the leader who led the inevitable battles. Washington, then, was the one who realized the Declaration. Therefore, "the new and just law" was for Shevchenko "Washington's new and just law."

We have attempted to present here some understanding of Shevchenko's exposure to and familiarity with American ideas and thought. We have also tried to demonstrate how Russian Communists have tried repeatedly to erase these facts from history. These very attempts at falsification, however, should not surprise the informed American reader. In the Soviet Union all liberal arts and sciences, fine arts, and literature have been under the dictatorship of the Russian Communist Party since 1922. American scholars (see the Symposium edited by Prof. C. E. Black, Princeton, "Re-writing Russian History," "Soviet Interpretations of Russia's Past," Frederick A. Praeger, 1956, 2d revised edition, 1962) analyzed how the principle of "Soviet Methods of Teaching History," expressed by M. A. Zinoviev, was realized in the field of history: "History is a powerful weapon of Communist education and it must wholly serve the cause of the struggle for communism."

The same principle was applied with even greater emphasis, however, to literature in the Soviet Union under the Russian Communist dictatorship; excellent evidence for this generally well-known fact is presented in the book by Maurice Friedberg *Russian Classics in Soviet Jackets* (New York and London: Columbia University Press, 1962. See also H. Swayze, *Political Control of Literature in the U.S.S.R., 1946-1959,* Russian Research Studies, 1962). If that happened in the Soviet Union with the classical Russian authors like Pushkin, Turgenev, and Tolstoy, one can imagine what happened and is happening to the Ukrainian Shevchenko. Like the great Russian writers, Shevchenko also was degraded to an adornment of Russian Communist tyranny by making him a weapon of ideological warfare in the service of specific Soviet ideals through the use of different techniques including tampering with the originals, as was done with letters of Chekov and Dostoevsky. What happened to Pasternak and Yevtushenko is also a good example.

The most important technique for the falsification of the ideas of Shevchenko is "Soviet Semantics."

The Russian Communists developed a "double talk" vocabulary, devised to mislead and confuse non-Communists, a real "up-side-down" language. For instance, the Communist meaning of the word "democracy" is actually our meaning of dictatorship; "liberation" means the Communist takeover of a free country; "aggressor" means any person or nation opposing Soviet imperialism; "militarism" means the creation of non-Communist armed strength; "colonialism" means possessing territory that Moscow wants, and so on.

In America only Norman Thomas was aware of this fact and warned of it in a good number of speeches. In substance he said, "The Communists plundered the whole terminology of European liberalism, democracy, and humanitarianism and changed their meaning into the very opposite." (See Roman Smal-Stocki, *Captive Nations,* 1960, Bookman Association, p. 44.)

It was of fundamental importance that our late President, John F. Kennedy, with his grasp of ideological conception in the conversations with Khrushchev in Vienna in 1961 immediately became aware of this fact. In his television report (*Time,* June 16, 1961) he publicly stated:

> "The facts of the matter are that the Soviets and ourselves give wholly different meanings to the same words: War, peace, democracy, and popular will. We have wholly different views of right and wrong, of what is an internal affair and of what is aggression. And, above all, we have wholly different concepts of where the world is and where it is going."

The Secretary of State Dean Rusk also warned Americans in his address at the National Press Club in Washington, D.C., on July 10, 1961:

> "The underlying crisis of our generation arises from the fact that the Soviet Union did not join the United Nations in fact, as well as in form, and lend itself to the commitments they and the rest of us made in the midst of a great war. The possession of power was transformed once more to ambition for more power.
>
> "The capacity to defy law became a contempt of law. Doctrines were revised and adopted to promote an imperialism as old as the tragic history of man. An entire people was sealed off from the rest of the world, and secrecy became a prime strategic weapon. The institutions of the international community were either ignored or undermined from within. In the process the very language of international

intercourse became distorted and contrived. 'Peace' became a word to describe whatever condition would promote their world revolution. 'Aggression' is whatever stands in its way. 'People's democracy' is a term applied to regimes no one of which has been chosen by free election. 'Self-determination' is loudly espoused but only in areas not under Communist control; the central issue of the crisis is the announced determination to impose a world of coercion upon those not already subjected to them." (U.S. News & World Report, July 24, 1961.)

Thus with their "up-side-down" language the Russian Communists created in the Soviet Union an ideological "up-side-down" Shevchenko. The best illustration for this tragic fact is the Shevchenko stamp issue of 1954 for the commemoration of the alliance of Hetman Chmelnicky with Muscovy's Tsar of 1654.

"Reunion" Stamps.

Taras Shevchenko damned Chmelnicky for this alliance with Muscovy. In contrast, he glorified Hetman Mazepa's fight for freedom of Ukraine and in his "Testament" called for a revolution against Russia:

> "Bury me thus I pray and rise!
> From fetters set you free
> And with your foe's unholy blood
> Baptize your liberty!"

(translation by C. H. Andrusyshen and Watson Kirkconnell in *Ukrainian Poets* Toronto University Press, 1963). This was the same Shevchenko, a champion of Washington, who was presented on these stamps as a champion of the union of Ukraine with Russia with the inscription "Ukraine's Reunion with Russia." These stamps constitute not only a falsification of all the ideas Shevchenko ever stood for but also include a historical falsification. In the year 1654 there did not exist a "Russia." Instead, there was only the Muscovite Tsardom.

T. Shevchenko's Daguerreotype taken in 1859.

## III

### *The Present Marxist-Leninist War Against George Washington*

WHAT AN amazing factor of current history is the present Shevchenko discussion in the Soviet Union which has been going on since the American Congress passed into law the erection of the Shevchenko monument in Washington, D.C. Some excerpts we quoted already.

The very fact that the movement for the erection of this statue of Taras Shevchenko met with bitter denunciations in Moscow and Kiev underscores the fact that the Communist rulers of Ukraine have grasped the meaning underlying this project. With admirable perception they know and appreciate the power of Shevchenko's ideas. Because they are unable to deny outright that Shevchenko was a powerful prophet of freedom and humanism, the Communist leaders have tried instead to deny to us, Americans of Ukrainian descent, the right to worship Shevchenko as our national hero. Toward this end the Soviet press has denounced this project to raise the monument in Washington as a "wily and ingenious tool of American imperialists" and their "servants, the Ukrainian bourgeois nationalists."

For example, one of the highest ranking poets in Ukraine today, Mykola Bazhan, wrote recently castigating the Americans of Ukrainian descent in the United States for their endeavors to honor Shevchenko on the forthcoming 150th anniversary of his birth in 1964:

> "The peoples of the Soviet Union," Bazhan wrote,[33] "and with them all progressive mankind are getting ready for a worthy observance of the immortal memory of the genius lover of freedom. . . .
>
> "But our enemies are not asleep. The American imperialists, relying on those docile servants, the Ukrainian nationalists, are planning to take advantage of the 150th anniversary for the monstrous, disgusting, and provocative purpose of slandering the homeland of Shevchenko, Soviet

> Ukraine, and our people with a flood of anti-Soviet insults, provocations, muck, lies, and distortions."

He went further to attack Professor Lev E. Dobriansky, Dr. D. Dontsov, and Professor P. Zaitsev, who allegedly committed "blasphemous falsifications" of Shevchenko's works, and who were blamed for attempting to present "our great poet as some kind of advocate of the modern 'American way of life.' "

> "The peoples of the world will firmly slap the dirty hands of the American politicians and nationalist Judases who are trying to besmirch the right arm of a pure human spirit, the spirit of truth and freedom, the spirit of goodness and just anger, the spirit of generosity and eternity, the spirit, image and word of Shevchenko."

These quotations are a sample of how the Russian Communists represent our work in this country on behalf of Taras Shevchenko as his anniversary approaches.

Of course, the American historians, the Kremlinologists, and Sovietologists are permitting these insults to pass by unchallenged because in the present field of Slavic and Soviet studies, which one might describe as being almost "directed and managed," the policy is delivered from the proper institutions and it is a policy of "co-existence." Therefore, everything which "endangers" the co-existence and the current "cultural" exchange programs must be glossed over in silence. But there are distinguished personalities of American and Canadian public life who, to the great anger of Moscow, know the facts about Shevchenko. Here are a few remarkable voices:

In commenting on the importance of Taras Shevchenko in the *Washington Star* (Oct. 13, 1963) Dr. Frederick Brown Harris, Chaplain of the U.S. Senate, had this to say:

> An outstanding Ukrainian poet who was a contemporary of Abraham Lincoln published a want ad that resounds across a hundred years. He died just after the man who saved the Union entered the White House to face black days. His name is Taras Shevchenko. He was and is the enduring voice of his valiant land in its age-long struggle for freedom. During his lifetime, most of which he spent in the slavery of serfdom, Ukraine was bound by the

> shackles of Tsarist tyranny. Shevchenko, in his inspired poetry, helped mightily to keep alive the dream of an independent Ukraine.
>
> With volcanic anger, defying the Russian handcuffs, his eyes were riveted with hope upon the American rebels who had revolted against the unjust exactions of a royal master and by their victory inspired all who longed to breathe freedom.
>
> These "American rebels" were American patriots of 1776 who, under the leadership of George Washington, attained freedom for the United States.

Another outstanding scholar who sees a close analogy between Lincoln and Shevchenko is Prof. Watson Kirkconnell, President of Acadia University in Wolfville, Nova Scotia, Canada. In a letter to the Shevchenko Memorial committee in rebuttal of the spurious charges by the *Washington Post* against the Shevchenko memorial, Professor Kirkconnell wrote:

> "More than any other man who ever lived, Shevchenko wrote and struggled for the freeing of the serfs in the old Russian Empire. The Imperial Decree abolished serfdom on the day of the poet's funeral and his name has always been inseparably associated with that birth of freedom. If one were to make a parallel with contemporary events in the U.S.A., one would have to imagine himself writing both 'John Brown's Body' and 'The Battle Hymn of the Republic' and then to imagine the liberation of the American slaves coming at this death, without any war whatever, by a great act of administrative assent. To the 45 million Ukrainians in the world today, Shevchenko is a brother of Abraham Lincoln."
>
> Thus in a wider and deeper sense, both Lincoln and Shevchenko are forerunners of modern champions of the present captive nations, champions for their liberation and freedom. American scholars are fully aware that like Abraham Lincoln, Taras Shevchenko was not a narrow nationalist. He was concerned not only over the oppression of the Ukrainian people by Moscow, but also over the oppression of the Poles, the Lithuanians, the Georgians, and the other ancient peoples who have been subjugated by an unbridled Russian imperialism, including the Jews.

> For both of them, Lincoln and Shevchenko, were men dedicated to the cause of justice and freedom according to the gospel.

On the occasion of the 90th anniversary of the First Ukrainian Academy of Liberal Arts and Sciences, of the Shevchenko Scientific Society, Inc., which was observed in 1963, there was held a Congress of Free Ukrainian Scholarship in New York City. Our late president John F. Kennedy sent to me, as President of the Congress and of the Society, the following telegram:

> My congratulations on the 90th anniversary of the Shevchenko Scientific Society, and on your sustained program for support for distinguished scholarship. Among your members have been some of the great names in learning to whom the world owes an incalculable debt. As you move into the decade which will culminate in your centennial, you have our best wishes and felicitations. May you continue to extend the frontiers of human knowledge in the years ahead.
>
> John F. Kennedy

This evaluation of our free scholarship under the banner of Taras Shevchenko in America also deeply disturbed the Muscovite Communists, and they intensified their attacks against the planned monument of Shevchenko in Washington, D.C.

But there was also another campaign begun in 1963. The *Washington Post* started a series of editorials as a smear campaign against the Shevchenko memorial, stating among other arguments that "Shevchenko did not know anything about America." The Russian Romanov monarchists, who although they are now American "citizens," still use their aristocratic titles in order to decorate as sons in law the children of American millionaires, joined the *Washington Post* in the protest campaign.[34]

Why did the Shevchenko-Washington issue become such an explosive issue for the Soviet Union? Why was such a "row" created in Washington, D.C. by the *Washington Post?* Why did the misled editor of the *Washington Post* invite the Ukrainian Communist delegate to the United Nations, Kizya, to enter into the controversy? Why did the Soviet embassy in Washington, D.C., enter into the controversy and why finally did the Soviet government order the complete elimination of any mention of George Washington in the article: *"Poet, Artist and Fighter for Freedom,"* on the occasion of the 150th anniversary of the birth of Taras Shevchenko, by Alexander Deitch, published in its official magazine *U.S.S.R.,* printed for distribution in U.S.A., March issue 1964? In the April, 1964 issue of *U.S.S.R.* the article of Academician Maxim Rylsky and Alexander Deitch "The Poetry of Taras Shevchenko" contains no mention of Washington. . . . Surely this is a special achievement of Russian specific diplomatic tact, but is this fact of silencing all American ties of Shevchenko not a falsification of his ideology? Did not the "big brother" contribute here an amazing method to the international UNESCO celebrations: "celebration by falsification"? Why this panic-stricken fear of the name of the Founding Father Washington?

The answers to these important questions are simple and can be found in the rather large bibliography on the ideas of the American Declaration of Independence, but specifically in the works of Professor Henry Steele Commager,[35] a distinguished authority on American history and the American Declaration of Independence, which, I repeat, was called "the new and just law of Washington" by Shevchenko more than a century ago.

Rebellion and revolution were the progenitors of the U.S.A., and the American Declaration of Independence was and still is for all oppressed, captive peoples the most subversive, revolutionary document ever written. It is even today, without the knowledge of our cold war strategists, an explosive rallying cry for revolutionists against tyranny, imperialism, and colonialism not only in Asia and Africa but, above all, among all Captive Nations inside and outside the Soviet Union which have contributed at least some 40 million American citizens to the United States which still maintain close links by innumerable family ties with their old nations and countries.

I will now list these revolutionary ideas I have been speaking of and list with them their Communistic counterparts: 1) that all men are created equal although the Russians claim they are "more equal" among Soviet nationalities as the imperial nation; 2) that all men have inalienable rights, a right to life, liberty, and the pursuit of happiness although these very rights were all liquidated in the Russian Communist police and terror state and do not exist in the Soviet Union; 3) that the purpose of government is just to secure these inalienable rights which in the Soviet Union were abolished and the whole population enserfed by the State, and most important of all, 4) that men have a right to overthrow the existing government and to form and establish a new and just government which would mean in the Soviet Union the right to an American-style democratic revolution against Russian Communist dictatorship.

All these principles embodied in the American Declaration of Independence are an indictment against Marxism-Leninism, against Russian Soviet imperialism and colonialism, and especially against the ideas of the Russian Communist party program of 1961,[36] as well as against Premier Nikita Khrushchev himself, once the old and trusted collaborator of Stalin.

It is true that Americans did not invent the above mentioned doctrines. They have European roots; some of them are even Jesuit originated. But what Americans did invent is the mechanism to realize them and to put them to work by written constitution, effective legal limitation of government, checks and balances through the division of power, and the possibility of judicial review of laws.

Thus the revolutionary evolution that followed the issuing of the Declaration of Independence gave Americans freedom and equality with no royalty, hereditary nobility, or military caste; a freedom which included especially religious freedom with no established church; a freedom which also included the idea of a classless society based on popular education of the masses.

Thus the United States, which, after the purchase of Alaska, practically bordered with the old Russian Empire, represented once the very antithesis of the Russian absolute divine right monarchy and of the Russian tyrannical imperialism over its colonies.

But in order to understand the present Shevchenko-Washington discord one must first grasp the fundamental fact that the United States with its Declaration of Independence is still today the very antithesis of the new Russian Empire, the Soviet Union. Behind the modernized phraseology of the present Communist ideology are hidden the three old pillars of the official ideology of Tsar Nicholas I—Russian divine right autocracy now adapted into Marxist-Leninist right autocracy; Russian official nationalism-chauvinism now encased in the concept of a "homogeneous" Soviet nation speaking the Russian language, and Russian orthodoxy now replaced by dialectical materialism as a new established state religion. This fact has been convincingly proved by Professors Noth, Monnerot, and Bochenski.[37]

There are in the American Declaration of Independence ideas which represent the most dangerous challenge for the Russian Soviet Empire and its Communistic ideology which has repressed several American "firsts" that were achieved by this unique revolution-born nation.

First, Americans were the first people to organize a revolution against their own mother country because of ideological reasons and thereby established for all people who accept the truths of these American ideas the right "to dissolve the political bands" which connect them with another and to assume . . . separate and equal status." This right is deeply felt by all non-Russian nations within the Soviet Union which regard Russia not at all as a "mother country" and which have no language, cultural, or traditional ties with Russia, but instead do have recollections of barbarian terror and oppression since Russian Tsarist times.

Secondly, even now an explosive inspiration and hope radiates from these memorable sentences, the more so as this right is basically founded in the Declaration of Independence on the right of revolution, the right to abolish and alter governments by the institution of constitutional conventions. This is another American "first."

Thirdly, as a consequence of this principle there followed a third American "first," the beginning of popular self-government based on the Jeffersonian faith: the ability and capacity of common men to govern themselves. This political philosophy attracted and still does attract millions of emigrants from Europe and all over the world because America has proved for the whole of mankind that self-government can work and work efficiently.

Fourthly, the most fundamental American "first" and one of vital importance for the understanding of current events is the fact that Americans were the first people to plan and create a nation by their own will and action as a deliberately planned application of ideas, intelligence, will, and revolutionary action. With the fanatical dedication of thinkers, statesmen, and soldiers, this creative elite whose first self-evident revolutionary truth was that "all men are created equal,"—politically, socially, economically equal—rallied the masses for the supreme task of nation-founding. They effected a great evolutionary program for the future and for the formation of the classless society which was so beautifully expressed by Shevchenko: "Bez cholopa i bez pana" which in English means "Without serfs and without masters."

Thus these ideas formed the American nationalism. They became as well the center, the so-called "holy ideas" of the American national consciousness which would eventually be hardened through sacrifice and struggle and finally would be attached to the symbolism expressed by the free eagle and the revolutionary theme of the American national anthem.

What is of the greatest import for our current history is that the Founding Fathers were deeply aware that the ideology of the new America as it was expressed in the Declaration had validity not only for Americans but for all mankind. This global outlook on the part of the Founding Fathers I choose to call "American Messianism" because it is obvious that these great men believed deeply in the victorious march of progress of these very ideas over all the world to challenge the Old World nationalism bit by bit.

In a letter commemorating the 50th anniversary of the American Declaration of Independence, Thomas Jefferson expressed in convincing terms what was in the mind of the Fathers:

> "May it be to the world what I believe it will be . . . the signal for arousing men to burst the chains under which monarch ignorance and superstition had persuaded them to

Woodcut of George Washington
honoring his bi-centennial birthday
anniversary by the government
of the Ukrainian People's Republic
in exile by Petro Cholodny, Jr.

bind themselves and to assume the blessings and security of self-government. All eyes are opened, or are opening to the rights of man. The general spread of the light of science has already laid open to every view the palpable truth that the mass of mankind has not been born with saddles on their backs, nor a favored few booted and spurred, ready to ride them legitimately . . . there are grounds for hope for others."

What a terrific challenge this eighteenth century "American Messianism" represented to the old Tsarist Russian Orthodox Messianism which was based on the "Moscow, the third Rome" legend! What an explosive challenge it still represents to the present Russian Communist imperialistic Messianism with its global goal of a World Soviet Union as well as to the non-Russian nations inside the Soviet Union and to all Captive Nations who were not "born with saddles on their backs. . . ."

The bearer of this American challenge, of this "American Messianism" to the old Russian Empire of Tsar Nicholas I, the "gendarme of Europe," became Taras Shevchenko who defended the freedom of Ukraine and the freedom as well of all oppressed peoples.

Shevchenko, a champion of Washington's Law, remains as a challenge to the present Russian Soviet imperialism and colonialism. Here in this fact, for all Americans to see, lies the hidden cause of this "row" which surrounds the erection of the statue of Taras Shevchenko in our nation's capital which has been fomented by the Russian Communist party in actions both inside the Soviet Union and in our country too.

It is a puzzling fact of contemporary American life that a man of the stature of Henry Steele Commager can generalize so freely about the moral implications of the freedoms and responsibilities described in the Declaration of Independence for contemporary Americans:[38]

> "With this unprecedented experience with nationalism, Americans should have the liveliest sympathy for those peoples throughout the globe who are today striving to create a nation. We were the first to show that it could be done and we should be the first to welcome others when they try to repeat our experience. . . ."

In writing this, Commager shows that he grasps the real situation and next he finds a parallel situation in Africa and Asia:

> The methods of this global revolution, too, are familiar enough. For it is one of the great paradoxes of history that the revolt of Asia and Africa against the "West" is being carried on with the tools and techniques devised by that West. The political instrument is Western nationalism; the social instrument is Western equality; the economic instrument is Western science and technology.

Commager holds that "Americans should be the first to sympathize with the impoverished millions of Asia and Africa."

And yet he sees no moral implications for Americans regarding the Captive Nations inside and outside the Soviet Union. He has no understanding for the processes going on among Captive

Nations, and he has not one single word of sympathy for them in his otherwise excellent article on the American Declaration. Commager fails to see the far stranger paradoxical struggle going on simultaneously with that of the tribes and peoples of Africa and Asia to gain nationhood in which some old nations in Europe are deprived of self-government, equality, and freedom by Russian Communist dictatorship. Among these deprived European nations which have been absorbed by the Soviet Empire are to be found even countries such as Poland, Czechoslovakia, and Yugoslavia which were allies of the United States during World War II!

Thus it seems that American scholarship is completely blind to the fate of the victims of Russian Soviet imperialism and to the still existing revolutionary challenge of the ideas of the American Declaration of Independence living within the hearts of the people within the Soviet Union in the 14 countries called "Union Republics" (three of these "Union republics"—Estonia, Latvia, and Lithuania—are not recognized by our government as parts of the U.S.S.R.;) they are also living in the hearts of the people of the 16 so-called "Autonomous Republics," of the six "Autonomous Regions," and 10 "National Areas" which go to make up together what we call "the Captive Nations."

The best proof that this challenge made by the revolutionary ideas of the American Declaration of Independence still exists inside the USSR can be found in this current "Shevchenko-Washington" discord which is being fomented inside the Soviet Union and by the actions of the agents Kizya and Dobrynin of the Russian Communist party in the United States.

We historians must explain how it could happen that the American nation, despite its profoundly revolutionary ideas and traditions, and after having absolute air superiority and the atomic weapons monopoly in the postwar period and with this monopoly the assurance of absolute superiority internationally, could practically abandon the ideology of its Founders and their expressed belief in the global validity of their ideological contribution?

The fire of "American Messianism" apparently burned out

and in the inevitable clash with "Russian Communist Messianism—imperialism" America has gradually retreated. . . .

How could it happen? What are the reasons for this retreat? In our opinion we must look for the causes of this spectacular retreat and the subsequent decline of American moral, political, and military prestige in the world in the transformation undergone by the old American ideological heritage which has turned it into a world outlook peculiar to a business civilization. Professor Henry Steele Commager is aware of it. What he is not aware of is the catastrophic consequences that decline in ideological commitment on the part of the United States has had for the fate of Central and Eastern Europe. Nor has Professor Commager considered the later consequences of these facts in Europe which have recently produced on the American continent the crises in Cuba, Panama, and Latin America. This transformation was clearly expressed by one of the recent successors of George Washington, Calvin Coolidge, when he said that "America's business is business."

In addition, the eminent American sociologist from Hungary, the late Professor Bela Kovrig, of Marquette university, Milwaukee, Wis., regarded the American nation as a "business community." According to Dr. Kovrig, the deep root of the fact that America was losing the leadership of the free world lies in the explanation that she lost the direction that had once been the key to the country's destiny. Even the present academic generation in America is shaped first and foremost not by the old American ideals but by relativism, especially in the moral field, by the belief that we are living in the post-religious and post-national age. Ours is a time when any nationalism, any patriotism is denounced as "tribalism." The old Russian Nihilism reached the shores of our country. . . .

These contemporary principles have undermined the old American patriotism-nationalism and have created a vacuum which, in many fields, has been filled by masterful Soviet propaganda about the Russian Communist "avante garde of humanity," the new Soviet man and the new Soviet civilization.

Since after World War II, there has been in the Soviet Union a terrifying development of a new Russian Soviet Nationalism-"Messianism," far more aggressive and imperialistic than anything we knew before World War I under the regime of the Tsars. While this is happening there we are facing in this nation an ideological vacuum especially among our young people. Our university students often can only answer a question like "Why are you an American?" either with surprised silence or with answers like "Because I was born here" or "Because we have a high living standard" or "Because we have social security. . . ." The old principles of our Founding Fathers have been forgotten.

What this cult of Soviet patriotism and imperialism is like in the Soviet Union is best illustrated in this short poem by Michael Lvov entitled: "Russia" (*Golos Rodiny,* No. 40 (537) May, 1961).

Russia—it's Lenin!
The October—It's swing!
Russian means Lenin
In acts and thoughts!

The pride of nations
The maturity of the epoch—
The Russia of rapidity,
The Russia of boldness.

We started to construct
The Russia of steel
The Russia of troika cells,
The Russia of machines.

Not a dream, not a misfit
Not the country of carts—
Russia means the Universe,
Russia means the epoch!

It is easy to see that in comparison with Lvov, Fjodor Tyutchev was a mere orphan with imperialistic dreams . . .

One can, therefore, fully understand the present "uproar in the Soviet Union," the uproar of Kizya and Dobrynin in the United States, both of which rail against the true interpretation of the Shevchenko-Washington programmatic and prophetic call and against the true symbolism of the monument of Shevchenko in Washington, D.C.

The Russian Communists fear that this monument will reawaken in Americans their old heritage, their old revolutionary ideas. The Russians fear that these American ideas which are permitted to embrace Africa and Asia, could penetrate behind the Iron Curtain into the Russian Soviet Empire and disturb the tyranny that is exercised over the colonial victims.

But the old revolutionary ideas of the Founding Fathers, nevertheless, are still at work in the Soviet Empire. It is just that a large part of the present generations of Americans do not wish to notice it. We here have other worries, they say, such as how can we feed Russian Communists with our grain.

There are fortunately still people in America who are dedicated to the old revolutionary ideas and let us hope that in the approaching world crisis they will defend the American ideological heritage.

By passing unanimously Public Law 86-749, the U.S. Congress has proved this convincingly to the whole world and all Captive Nations.

Marx stated in 1848 in his "Communist Manifesto": "A specter is haunting Europe—the specter of Communism." We have seen in the preceding pages that truly "A specter is haunting Russian Communism—the specter of George Washington and Shevchenko."

## IV

### *America Meets the First Shevchenkoite: Father Honcharenko*

THE modern space research beams by special apparatus vibrating rays to the planets of our solar system and gets back an echo in the sender's place and country. Ideas as well have the power to radiate in this manner from the place of their conception all over the world and then, finally to echo homeward.

The American Declaration of Independence and its ideas have been and still are radiating throughout the entire world. Upon hearing these ideas many became champions of the American ideal by joining in the struggle for their realization in the American Revolutionary War. Men like LaFayette, Steuben, Kosciuszko, and Pulaski were reached by the American ideological "beams" and came to America to fight for the ideas of the American Declaration of Independence. Others, like Shevchenko, were later reached by these same ideas but remained in their native countries proclaiming to their fellow countrymen Washington's "new and just law." These radiated American beams to foreign countries soon started to return to America in the form of political emigrations of many fighters for freedom and champions of the new law: America, for these men, was a refuge in their fight against tyranny.

We have earlier in this paper presented facts about how Taras Shevchenko came in contact on four occasions with America and its spirit while still living in the Russian Empire. But when did America meet here on her own soil the first Ukrainian who was a Shevchenko enthusiast in search of that freedom promised by "Washington's law" which Shevchenko praised so highly?

The first man who represented the direct response to the radiation of "Washington's new and just law" from Shevchenko's Ukraine to the U.S.A. was the Reverend Ahapius Honcharenko (1832-1916).

It is true that Father Honcharenko was not the first Ukrainian to reach American soil. Some trace the date of this back to Capt. John Smith, the founder of the English settlement in Jamestown, Virginia, who is known to have travelled through Ukrainian lands in 1603 and to have brought to America settlers with Ukrainian surnames like Bohun, Nemyrych, Hrabowsky, and others.

But Father Honcharenko was the first Ukrainian who grew up in the Shevchenko era and was dedicated to the Shevchenko ideology. He was born in the Kiev province of Ukraine, in a Cossack family. Educated in the Kiev Theological academy, he became a deacon. Still in the seminary, Honcharenko became an enthusiast of Shevchenko and the principles of the Sts. Cyril and Methodius Brotherhood, and he felt a mission to continue Shevchenko's fight against Russian Tsarism. As an excellent linguist who by the end of his lifetime had mastered, besides Ukrainian and Russian, old and modern Greek, Latin, Hebrew, Arabic, Italian, and English, he was sent to Greece in a Russian Theological mission attached to the Russian Embassy in 1857. He contacted by mail Alexander Herzen,[39] the famous Russian exile and publisher of the "Northern Star" and "The Bell," and who was a promoter of the Decembrist traditions. A fighter for the emancipation of the serfs in Russia, Herzen was also the initiator of the "Land and Freedom" movement and the founder of populism.

Father Honcharenko became a secret contributor to "The Bell," the London-based magazine published by Herzen, and later authored among other things the eulogy which appeared in that magazine for Shevchenko. He also attacked serfdom, especially as it existed for the Church-owned serfs, and absolutism. Russian spies discovered this link between the priest and Herzen, and he was arrested to be brought home for trial. He was fortunate enough to escape, then went to London in 1860 to join Herzen's circle. He became acquainted with Nicholas Ogarev, Michael Bakunin, also with Giuseppi Garibaldi (1807-1882), and Giuseppi Mazzini (1805-1872), as well as other revolutionaries. He worked in the British museum as a classifier of numismatics and as a teacher.

As the Russian liberal leadership then consisted of atheists, Honcharenko left Herzen and joined the religious Italians who were the leaders of the "Young Italy" movement. Mazzini had also given him addresses and recommendations to introduce him to revolutionary friends in America. This surely was the origin of Father Honcharenko's plan to emigrate to the United States.

But before leaving for America he returned to his beloved adopted country, Greece, where he accepted Greek citizenship, visited Hermopolis where he published a Latin-Greek Lexicon, and went also to Smyrna where the Polish exiles welcomed him with a banquet, and then to the famous Orthodox Mount Athos. At this final stop he was ordained a priest and he then made a pilgrimage to Jerusalem. The Russian Bishop and Consul there attempted to have Honcharenko arrested, but the Russian Catholic Prince, Ivan Gagarin,[40] protected him through the Catholic Patriarch, Calerggi, and helped him to obtain a teaching position in the Jesuit school at Ghazik, Lebanon. The Russian consul and his spies forced Father Honcharenko to flee through Syria to Alexandria but while there, the Russian consul, Lagodowsky, hired gangsters to kill him. The priest was only wounded in the attack, but, when the hired killer was caught, he confessed that he was in the pay of the Russian consul. Father Honcharenko returned to Athens. Even there he felt in danger from the Russian intelligence service and so he decided to emigrate to the United States.

On January 1, 1865 Father Honcharenko arrived in Boston on the "Yarington" and went immediately to New York City. There the Greek consul took him under his protection, and appointed him priest to the Orthodox Greeks in that area. He lectured at St. John's Theological seminary, collaborated with the Bible Society in an Arabic translation of the Bible, and translated the New Testament into Church-Slavic. He even established his own printing shop. He was often invited to celebrate Holy Mass in many cities as far away as New Orleans. As Orthodox priests may marry, Father Honcharenko found among the Italian friends of Mazzini in Philadelphia an American girl, Albina Citti, and they were married in 1865.

In 1867 Alaska was sold to the United States and Father Honcharenko expressed the desire to be with the free people of Alaska because he suspected that many of the so-called "Russians" there were political Ukrainian exiles. Therefore, he hoped through these people in Alaska to reach the political exiles in Siberia. He gradually developed the plan that America should also acquire Siberia and coupled with Alaska the United States could form a buffer state to protect itself from Russian imper-

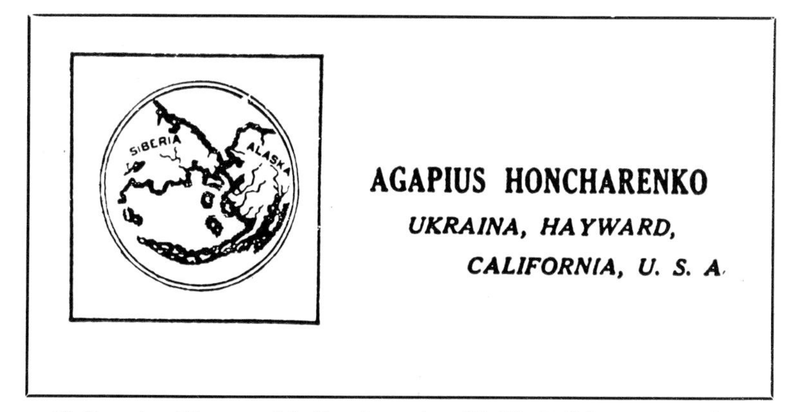


Visitcarde of Reverend A. Honcharenko with His Political Conception of a Union of Siberia with Alaska.

ialism which he expected soon again to expand in the direction of North America.

Father Honcharenko established a contact with the Secretary of State, William H. Seward, the initiator of the purchase of Alaska, and went to Washington, D.C. His "Russian and English Phrase Book for Traders, Travellers, and Teachers," was published with government funds for military personnel in Alaska in 1868. He also got from the Secretary of State the promise of a subsidy for the publication of a bi-lingual paper for the citizens of Alaska.

The priest left with his wife for San Francisco, the gateway to the West, and soon after arriving in California, began organizing the Sts. Cyril and Methodius Brotherhood. He also established the first Orthodox church there and started publishing the *Alaska Herald* in 1868 and later in 1873 the *Alaska Herald-Svoboda* (*Liberty*). In the newspaper's first issue Father Honcharenko published in English an article titled "Curious Ideas of the Poet Taras Shevchenko" and in the second issue there followed excerpts from the revolutionary poems of Shevchenko

ESTABLISHED MARCH 1, 1868.

# Alaska Herald.

VOL. 1 SAN FRANCISCO, MARCH 1, 1868 No. 1

THE ALASKA HERALD

SUBSCRIPTIONS AND ADVERTISEMENTS CAN BE LEFT AT THE

PRINTING OFFICE OF CUBERY & CO

*SAN FRANCISCO, CALIFORNIA.*

SUBSCRIPTIONS.

INTRODUCTORY

Издатель Пресвитеръ Агапій Гончаренко.

THE CONSTITUTION OF THE UNITED STATES OF AMERICA

The first copy of "Alaska Herald" with a translation of the U.S.A. Constitution.

in the Ukrainian language. This was the first time that Shevchenko's name was mentioned on American soil.

Father Honcharenko managed to organize among the exiles in Siberia a secret distribution of 500 copies of his newspaper—a paper that was totally dedicated to the waging of a "Cold War" against Russian absolutism and imperialism, to the popularization of the American way of life, and of the American Constitution, which was translated in the first issue of the first paper. This Ukrainian immigrant to America is credited with popularizing the American Constitution throughout Siberia. . . .

The Tsarist Russian Government was immediately alarmed and sent to San Francisco for a counteraction a special Russian priest who had financial assistance from the Tsar to build the second Orthodox church there, one that was loyal to the Russian Tsar. This was in 1868.

Naturally, the Russian Tsarist regime became alarmed by the activities of Father Honcharenko because there were in exile in Siberia rather large groups of revolutionaries from all the captive and oppressed nations of the Russian Empire, especially from Poland and Ukraine. The priest had boldly written in his newspaper in 1870 that: "It (this paper) is published in order that the Sibiriaks (the population of Siberia) may hear over the ocean the free serene song from free America."

The anti-Tsarist articles of the *Alaska Herald-Svoboda* were used repeatedly by the Russian Embassy in Washington for protests at the Department of State. The English printed articles enlightened the American public opinion about the Russian feudal Empire, its absolutism, the oppression of the non-Russian peoples, and the crimes committed by the regime against the common people.

In many articles which were concerned with specifically Ukrainian problems, the priest-editor would publish excerpts from Shevchenko's poetry condemning the Tsar. In fact, his paper was, besides being the first Slavic paper to be published in America, the first Slavic tri-lingual paper to be published here. It appeared with not only Russian and Ukrainian, but Serbian as well as English contributions.

Honcharenko also organized the first Slavic Library in America which was later donated to the Bencroft Library.

In 1872 he sold his printing shop and became after 1873 quite active as a member of the highly respected California Academy of Sciences.

Summing up his own life experiences, he wrote in 1872: "During my last 12 years since my emigration of all the Slavic nationalities which I have met, only the Ukrainians and Poles were mature enough for self-government and democratic rule."[41] He bought a 50 acre farm which he called "Ukraina"; his cottage there he called "Svoboda" or "Liberty." He also built a chapel there; his wife conducted Sunday school, and he enjoyed the old Ukrainian specialty, an apiary. After the death of his wife, he was grief-stricken and died soon afterward in 1915.

During his whole life Father Honcharenko protected and helped all political escapees from Siberia or Sakhalin and petitioned the American government not to extradite them. He also defended the local population of Alaska against the monopoly exploitation by the Alaskan Commercial company and showed great feeling for social justice always practicing Christian charity. "Brotherly love and the rights of all is our cherished motto and will be the principle of our loyalty as American citizens," he wrote in his recollections which were published by Ukrainians under Austrian rule with whom he established close contact.

Honcharenko had many distinguished American friends: Horace Greeley, Charles A. Dana, Eugene Schuyler (the later Ambassador to Russia had learned to speak the Russian language from the priest), Hamilton Fish, George Kennan, General Halleck, Henry George, A. P. Swinford, and James Gordon Bennett.

And from free America he prepared "Fourth of July Letters" for his Ukrainian people in Kiev. "How long," he wrote, "before you in Russia will be able to celebrate your Fourth of July, a free press, and free religion? How long, my countrymen, will it be before you receive these things?" An American journalist, George C. Mansfield, who had visited Honcharenko in the Hayward Hills, wrote about these letters in the *San Francisco Chronicle* on July 23, 1905.[42]

Thus Honcharenko worked his whole life for the aim of a Fourth of July for Ukraine. That, indeed, would be the realization of Washington's "new and just law" as it was glorified by Taras Shevchenko!

America did not completely forget this devoted adopted son. In 1944 a "liberty ship" of the United States was named "Honcharenko."

Surely, Father Honcharenko is an outstanding and colorful personality in American history, who contributed to America's progress. Continuous persecutions, shadowing, attacking by the

Reverend A. Honcharenko in Alaska.

Tsarist spies, and even harrassment by foreign service agents did not break him. He conducted his own continuous "cold war" against imperialist Russia in the name of the ideas of the American Declaration of Independence and of our American Constitution. With his newspaper he was able to carry this fight into Siberia and through an extensive correspondence into his native Ukraine. Because all of his struggle was directed not only against Russian absolutism but also against Russian imperialism and colonialism and for the liberty of the oppressed captive nationalities, Honcharenko's name has been systematically disregarded in the publications of the history of Russia which have been published in recent years in America by the Russian imperialist school of East European history.

This is an injustice to his memory for these reasons:

(1) the same action which wealthy Herzen conducted against Russian absolutism and imperialism with his "The Bell" newspaper from London in the West and financed by his own money was duplicated by Honcharenko against Tsarism from America through Siberia. This great achievement was done almost entirely through Honcharenko's own earnings which only served to emphasize the priest-editor's dedication to the spirit of Shevchenko, to the principles of the Cyrilo-Methodian Brotherhood, and even to the Southern Decembrist traditions.

(2) Honcharenko's contacts with the leaders of "Young Italy," a part of the "Young Europe movement," are most interesting and deserve to be further investigated.

(3) He elaborated on the concept of a "free Siberia" which is still worthy of discussion.

(4) His courageous struggle for social justice for the workers and native population of Alaska and his fight against the monopoly of one trading company is quite remarkable.

(5) He gave America its first English-Slavic language newspaper. In addition, he also organized the first Slavic Library, built the first Orthodox church in the San Francisco area, and he was, in fact, the first American Slavicist of Slavic descent. Furthermore, Father Honcharenko published the first Old Church Slavic Bible in the United States.

Nevertheless he is ignored by the Russian imperialistic historians in the United States because he was really an American democrat propagating the application of American principles to the Russian Empire. He called his farm "Ukrainia," his home "Svoboda" which means "Liberty," and he always insisted, "I am not a Russian."

This American citizen found not even a note in the *Encyclopedia Americana* or in the *Dictionary of National Biography.*

But I do have hope that the younger generation of Americans will do him justice. If not because of these enumerated reasons, then possibly for the following pragmatic reasons: when after purchase of Alaska started public criticism against the federal government, criticism which held that "Alaska is good for nothing," that "Alaska is nothing but rocks and ice," that "there is no population except a few Indians and no resources in the country,"—then Honcharenko spoke out in his newspaper, the *Alaska Herald,* to silence the opposition by announcing on Oct. 15, 1868 for the first time the news that there is "gold in Alaska!" He wrote: "Gold is found both on the main peninsula and on the peninsula east of Cooks Inlet. The native women wear necklaces composed of beads of gold strung on string. No mining has been done, but lumps are simply picked from the surface of the earth. Coal and copper are known to exist in rich paying veins. When we are in receipt of definite information, we will give out the cheering cry of 'Gold!' We are already certain of the existence, but must await the results of the first pioneer mining company." According to the *Encyclopedia Americana,* the panning of gold in one single year in Alaska brought in $40 million.

Honcharenko himself and his faithful American-Italian wife died penniless.

From the political point of view, it is easy to see that the isolationist America of Honcharenko's time did not understand him. He is not the first nor the last naturalized American citizen who was wasted by American political shortsightedness.

## NOTES

[1] Sir Edward S. Creasy, *The Fifteen Decisive Battles of the World* (1st ed.; London: 1851). He was a professor at London university.

[2] See: Nicholas Riazanovsky, *Nicholas I and Official Nationality in Russia* (Berkeley: University of California Press, 1959).

[3] A good presentation of Nicholas' Russia is in Marquis de Custine's *La Russie en 1839* (3rd ed.; Paris: 1846). The author visited Russia, had conversations even with Nicholas himself, and later wrote: "D'autres nations ont supporté l'oppression. La nation Russe l 'a aimée; elle l'aime encore." Vol. 3, p. 295.

[4] Eugene Pyziur, *The Doctrine of Anarchism of Michael A. Bakunin.* Marquette Slavic Studies, No. 1 (Milwaukee: Marquette University Press, 1955).

[5] Anatole G. Mazour, *Tsarist Russia and Communist* (Princeton, N. J.; D. Van Nostram Co., 1962) p. 224.

[6] Hans Kohn, *Mind of Russia,* p. 95.

[7] Richard Hare, *Pioneers of Russian Social Thought* (London: Oxford University Press, 1951) p. 130.

[8] Hans Kohn, *Pan-Slavism,* p. 127.

[9] Roman Smal-Stocki, *Shevchenko and the Jews.* Paper No. 20. Shevchenko Scientific Society, New York, N.Y., 1959.

[10] Pavlo Zaytsev, *Life of Taras Shevchenko* in Ukrainian, (Ukrainian Studies, New York-Paris: 1955) pp. 58-9.

[11] Allen Johnson, *The Dictionary of American Biography* (New York: Charles Scribners & Son, 1928) pp. 160-1. "Ira Frederick Aldridge, a Negro tragedian, was probably born in New York City although his birthplace is also given as Belair, near Baltimore, Md. Accounts of his early life are conflicting. His father, Joshua Aldridge, is variously described as a Negro ship-carpenter and as a full-blooded African chieftain who had been brought to America, educated, and settled as a pastor over a Colored church. It is stated that young Aldridge was educated in Schenectady, N.Y. and Glasgow, Scotland. According to the usual account, when Edmund Kean made his first visit to America, Ira Aldridge became his personal attendant and later accompanied him back to England where, encouraged by Kean, he studied for the stage. He made his debut in 1826 as Othello with considerable success. Highly praised by Kean, and nicknamed the "African Roscius," he was next seen at the Coburg and other metropolitan theaters, afterward touring the English and Irish provinces. At some time subsequent to 1830 Aldridge appeared unsuccessfully at the Mud theater in Baltimore. Returning to London, he played at Covent Garden (1833), the Lyceum, and the Surrey. His last London engagements were in 1858 and 1865. Among his roles were Othello, Lear, Macbeth, Aaron in "Titus Andronicus," Zanga in "The Revenge," Gambia in "The Slave," Rolla in 'Pizarro," and Mungo in "The Padlock." He was generally regarded as one of the ablest and most faithful interpreters of Shakespeare of his day. In 1853 he went to the Continent. Playing in Switzerland and Germany, crowded

houses greeted him everywhere. Honors, orders, and medals were showered upon him. For the last ten years of his life he played mainly on the Continent where he accumulated a considerable fortune. His wife was a white woman. He died in Lodz, Poland, while on his way to fill an engagement in St. Petersburg. He was a member of the Imperial and Archducal Order of Our Lady of the Manger in Austria, and an honorary member of the Imperial Academy of Fine Arts in St. Petersburg.

[12] I must mention here that contrary to the present policy in the Soviet Union racial antagonism against Africans was unknown in old Muscovy. Hannibal, an Ethiopian slave who served as a page of Tsar Peter I, married a girl of the Russian aristocracy and, since that time, a small amount of African ancestry is in many Russian aristocratic families who are proud of this fact indeed. The national poet of the Muscovites, Alexander Pushkin, was the great-grandson of this Hannibal.

[13] Marie Trommer-Trembicka, "Ira Aldridge, American Negro, and Taras Shevchenko, Poet of Ukraine," in *The Russian Review,* Oct., 1939. This article was reprinted in the *Svoboda Ukrainian Weekly* on April 18, 22, 29, 1961.

[14] Paul Robeson is a leading Communist among Afro-Americans. See the article by George E. Sokolsky: "Robeson Proclaims Self Enemy of U.S." which appeared in the *Milwaukee Sentinel* Dec. 6, 1960. "Robeson said that, if there was war between Russia and America, he would be on the side of the Soviet Union 'which would win—and should win.' "

[15] Bohdan Krawciw, "When Will Our Waiting for Washington Be Fulfilled," (in Ukrainian) *Svoboda,* No. 45, Apr. 10, 1961.

[16] W. Porsky, "Shevchenko and Washington" (in Ukrainian), *Nashe Zhyttia,* 1946.

[17] Excerpts From the Diary of Pelagja Rosciszewska," *The Annals of the Ukrainian Academy for Free Arts and Sciences,* I, 1 (New York: 1951). Serge Muravjov-Apostol (1796-1826) was a descendant on his mother's side of the Ukrainian Hetman, Danylo Apostol. Educated in Paris and St. Petersburg, he played a leading role in the conspiracies of the "Union of Liberation" and the "Southern Society." As Colonel of the Cherynhiv Regiment, he headed the mutiny of his regiment and, after the failure of the Decembrist Revolt, was sentenced to death together with Ryleev, P. Pestel, and Michael Bestuzhev-Rjumin (1803-1826) who was a second lieutenant in the Poltava Regiment and liaison to Polish revolutionary societies.

*Bignonia Catalpa,* the supposed beloved tree of Washington, was brought to Europe from North America and was widely cultivated in Poland and Ukraine. It is a decorative tree with bell-shaped flowers.

We could not find any material to support this East European tradition that this tree was in fact a beloved favorite of Washington. We assume that it was brought from America to Poland and Ukraine and here developed this legend by the association: American tree—Washington's tree. Perhaps the following explanation can give some direction. For it we are indebted to our distinguished colleague, Rev. Raphael Hamilton, S.J., professor of history, Marquette University, Milwaukee, Wis.:

In 1932 the Bicentennial Commission, appointed to celebrate the birth of George Washington, had extensive research done which was published as: "Honor to George Washington and Readings About George Washington." There on pages 97-8 Father Hamilton found that the only tree which the Commission is sure was planted by Washington and which still flourishes on the grounds of his home, Mt. Vernon, is a magnolia tree which the dictionary establishes to be very much the same as the bignonia tree. Both have large decorative leaves and white, pink, or red blossoms.

[18] See Tadeusz Butkiewicz, Taras Shevchenko and Zygmunt Sierakowski, *Ukrainian Historical Journal,* (Kiev: History Institute of the Academy of Sciences of the Ukrainian S.S.R., 1961) No. 1.

[19] Nicholas Berdyaev, *The Origins of Russian Communism* (London: Geoffrey Bles, 1948) p. 120.

[20] A. Nikowski, *Vita Nova* (Kiev: 1918) p. 8.

[21] Roman Smal-Stocki, "The Stature of Shevchenko in the Past and Present," *Ukrainian Studies* (Philadelphia: Shevchenko Scientific Society, 1962) IX, 17.

[22] V. Vynnychenko, *Rebirth of the Nation* (in Ukrainian) pp. 270-1.

[23] M. Liubchenko, "The Red Christ" in *In Memory of Shevchenko* (1920), (in Ukrainian).

[24] V. Koriak, *The Battle for Shevchenko* (Charkiv: 1925) pp. 45-6, (Ukr.).

[25] Petro Odarchenko, "Shevchenko in Soviet Literary Criticism," in *Taras Shevchenko, 1814-1861, a Symposium,* ed. by Volodymyr Mijakowsky and George Y. Shevelov (Gravenhage: Mouton Co., 1962).

[26] See Petro Odarchenko, *op. cit.,* p. 268.

[27] Petro Odarchenko, *op. cit.,* p. 270.

[28] Petro Odarchenko, *op. cit.,* pp. 287-8.

[29] Petro Odarchenko, *op. cit.,* p. 301.

[30] Bohdan Krawciw, *op. cit.,* p. 4.

[31] D. Ostrianyn, "The Great Ukrainian Thinker and Revolutionary Democrat," in *Kommunist Ukrainy,* No. 2, Feb., 1961; pp. 71-81. It is worthwhile to remember how the Russian Communists also used the name of Shevchenko for "Agitprop" purposes during the Spanish Civil War (1937-8). They organized a "Taras Shevchenko Company" and thus attracted Ukrainian Communists from America, France, and even western Ukraine. In a similar way they abused the names of the bard of Poland, Adam Mickiewicz, of Abraham Lincoln, and of others whose names were used as titles of companies or even brigades.

[32] Leonid Novychenko, "Shevchenko and They" in *Literaturna Gazeta,* Mar. 7, 1961, pp. 1-3.

[33] Mykola Bazhan in *Literaturna Ukraina,* Apr. 16, 1963.

[34] See: *Shevchenko, A Monument to the Liberation, Freedom, and Independence of All Captive Nations,* Remarks by Various Members of Congress in the House of Representatives, Nov. 13, 14, 20, and 2.; Dec. 4, 6, 1963; and Jan. 9, 13, 1964. U.S. Government Printing Office Washington: 1964.

[35] From the many books in this field, which have made the understanding of America easier for us, exiled European university professors, I men-

tion only the admirable publications of Henry Steele Commager: *Documents of American History,* 1944; *Living Ideas in America,* 1952; *The Great Declaration* (with R. B. Morris), 1958; *The Spirit of '76,* the *Great Proclamation,* 1960. Also see: Nathan Schachner, *The Founding Fathers,* 1963, and Carl Becker, *The Declaration of Independence,* 1963.

[36] *The Communist Blueprint for the Future* with an Introduction by Thomas P. Whitney (New York: E. P. Dutton & Co., 1962).

[37] J. Monnerot, *Sociologie du Communisme* (Paris: 1954); G. Noth, *Christentum und Kommunismus in der Weltwende* (Stuttgart: 1954), and J. Bochenski, *Der Sowjetrussische Dialektische Materialismus* (Bern: 1950).

[38] Henry Steele Commager, "Our Declaration Is Still a Rallying Cry," in *The New York Times Magazine,* July 2, 1961.

[39] Herzen had among the Russian liberals an honest approach to Ukraine's aspirations for freedom. In his "The Bell" (No. 34, 1837, p. 274), Herzen wrote: "What must we do if Ukraine, remembering all the oppressions of the Russians, serfdom, the recruitment, the injustice, the pillage, the knout . . . will desire to be neither under Poland nor under Russia? In my opinion the problem has to be solved simply: We have to recognize Ukraine as a free, independent country." See also Yar Slavutych, "Alexander Herzen and Ukraine," (*Ukrainian Quarterly,* XVI, No. 4, 1960).

[40] Prince Ivan Gagarin (1814-1882), Russian diplomat and convert to Catholicism in 1842, entered the Society of Jesus in 1843." *The Catholic Encyclopedia and the Encyclopedia Americana.*

[41] In the *Alaska Herald-Svoboda,* 1872.

[42] Other literature on Agapius Honcharenko: W. Luciw and Th. Luciw, Ahapius Honcharenko: Alaska Man (Toronto: Slavia Library, 1963); Y. *Czyzh, Andrij Ahapij Honcharenko* in the *Calendar Svoboda* (Jersey City: 1957), and H. H. Bancroft, *History of Alaska, 1730-1885* (San Francisco: A. L. Bancroft, 1886).

## THE SLAVIC INSTITUTE OF MARQUETTE UNIVERSITY

The Slavic Institute was established at Marquette University in 1949:

1. to foster the study of the history, culture, and civilization of the Slavic nations through the organization of courses, research, symposiums, seminars, public conferences, and publications.

2. to develop an appreciation of and preserve the cultural heritage of more than 14 million American citizens of Slavic descent in the spirit of the fundamental equality of all Slavic nations.

3. to strengthen American-Slavic cultural relations through original contributions to American scholarship.

The views expressed in the paper[illegible]e Slavi[illegible]stitute are those of their authors, and are [illegible] con[illegible]ed as representing the point of view of the Slavic [illegible]

## THE SLAVIC INSTITUTE OF MARQUETTE UNIVERS[illegible]

## PUBLICATIONS OF THE SLAVIC INSTITUTE

### MARQUETTE SLAVIC STUDIES

Pyziur, Eugene: The Doctrine of Anarchism of Michael A. Bakunin (1955).

Kamenetsky, Ihor: Hitler's Occupation of Ukraine—Study in Totalitarian Imperialism—1941-44 (1956).

Manning, Clarence A.: History of Slavic Studies in the United States (1957).

Kononenko, Konstantyn: Ukraine and Russia—A History of the Economic Relations Between Ukraine and Russia—1654-1917 (1958)

Mikus, Joseph: Slovakia:



### IN PROCESS

Meysztowicz, Very Rev ... in Poland 996-1386.

### PAPERS OF THE SLAV

No. 1: "Definition of ... Wisconsin-Milwaukee.

No. 2: "Origin of Natio ... sity.

No. 3: "Titoism" by Mi ... n.

No. 4: "Gomulka-ism" ... n.

No. 5: "National Comn ... ccount by Bela Kovrig, Mar

No. 6: "Should Commu ... uette University.

No. 7: "A Survey of S ... Wisconsin High School."—

No. 8: "The Problems ... nal-Stocki, Marquette Unive

No. 9: "The Scheme of

No. 10: "The Diplomatic ... errence J. Barragy.

No. 11: "The Slavic Ins ... tocki and Alfred J. Sokolni

No. 12: "Pushkin's Dedi ... F. Pauls, University of Cin

No. 13: "The Jews in the ... ign Affairs Department of th

No. 14: "The So-Called ... Scientific Society, Inc., Ne

No. 15: "Some Problem ... al Times" by Arnold Spekke.

**No. 16: "The Problem of Unity of World Communism" by Dinko A. Tomasic, University of Indiana.**

**No. 17: "Klonowicz and Ukraine: An Introduction to the Poem Roxolania"** by Marian Moore **Coleman.**

**No. 18: "Shevchenko Meets America"** by Roman Smal-Stocki, Marquette University.

No. 19: "The Slavs Between East and West" by Francis Dvornik, Harvard University.